The Archaeology of Islands

Archaeologists have traditionally considered islands as distinct physical and social entities. In this book, Paul Rainbird discusses the historical construction of this characterisation and questions the basis
for such an understanding of island archaeology. Through a series of
case studies of prehistoric archaeology in the Mediterranean, Pacific,
Baltic and Atlantic seas and oceans, he argues for a decentring of
the land in favour of an emphasis on the archaeology of the sea and,
ultimately, a new perspective on the making of maritime communities. The archaeology of islands is thus unshackled from approaches
that highlight boundedness and isolation, and is replaced with a new
set of principles – that boundaries are fuzzy, islanders are distinctive
in their expectation of contacts with people from over the seas and
island life can tell us much about maritime communities. Debating
islands, thus, brings to the fore issues of identity and community
and a concern with Western construction of other peoples.

Paul Rainbird is Head of Department and Senior Lecturer in Archaeology at the University of Wales, Lampeter. A Fellow of the Society
of Antiquaries and a Fellow of the Royal Anthropological Institute,
he is the author of *The Archaeology of Micronesia* and he serves on
the editorial boards of the *Journal of Island and Coastal Archaeology*
and *Research in Archaeological Education*.

TOPICS IN CONTEMPORARY ARCHAEOLOGY

Series Editor
RICHARD BRADLEY *University of Reading*

This series is addressed to students, professional archaeologists and academics in related disciplines in the social sciences. Concerned with questions of interpretation rather than the exhaustive documentation of archaeological data, the studies in the series take several different forms: a review of the literature in an important field and outline of a new area of research or an extended case study. The series is not aligned with any particular school of archaeology. While there is no set format for the books, all the books in the series are broadly based, well written and up to date.

The Archaeology of Islands

PAUL RAINBIRD

University of Wales, Lampeter

CAMBRIDGE
UNIVERSITY PRESS

CAMBRIDGE UNIVERSITY PRESS
Cambridge, New York, Melbourne, Madrid, Cape Town, Singapore, São Paulo

Cambridge University Press
32 Avenue of the Americas, New York, NY 10013-2473, USA

www.cambridge.org
Information on this title: www.cambridge.org/9780521853743

First published 2007

Printed in the United States of America

A catalog record for this publication is available from the British Library.

Library of Congress Cataloging in Publication Data
Rainbird, Paul.
The Archaeology of Islands / Paul Rainbird.
    p.   cm.   – (Topics in contemporary archaeology)
Includes bibliographical references and index.
ISBN 978-0-521-85374-3 (hardback)
ISBN 978-0-521-61961-5 (pbk.)
1. Islands.   2. Island archaeology.   3. Maritime anthropology.
I. Title.   II. Series.
GF61.R35   2007
930.10914′2–dc22   2007003875

ISBN   978-0-521-85374-3 hardback
ISBN   978-0-521-61961-5 paperback

For Sarah and Cerys

Contents

Figures

Acknowledgments

My colleagues and students at the University of Wales, Lampeter
have provided a stimulating environment in which to pursue the
issues raised in this book and I thank them for this. Penny Dransart
took on my onerous administrative duties while I took the time to
write this book and I thank her very much for that.

I would like to thank the series editor, Richard Bradley, and
Simon Whitmore, formerly of Cambridge University Press, for their
support of this project.

Parts of Chapter 2 and Chapter 4 have their origin in a paper
I published in the *Journal of Mediterranean Archaeology* (Rainbird
1999a). Parts of this paper have been modified and expanded here
while in other sections the details remain in the journal paper and are
referenced to indicate this. I would like to again take the opportunity
to thank John Cherry and Bernard Knapp, the editors of *JMA*, for
their help in improving that paper and providing the forum for

preliminary discussions of the issues pursued more extensively in this book.

Much of Chapter 3 and therefore the issues that are core to the argument in this book were presented at a workshop on 'Embodied Histories: Bodies, Senses, Memories in Archaeology & Anthropology' at Southampton University. I thank Andy Jones, Yannis Hamilakis and Eleanor Breen for commenting on a draft of the paper that forms the starting point for this chapter. I would also like to acknowledge valuable discussions with Mark Pluciennik on this topic.

The hospitality I have received in Scandinavia has been overwhelming and I wish to thank Goran Burenhult, Gunilla Hallin-Lawergren, Inger Österholm, Paul Wallin, Helen Wallin-Martisson and Olaf Winter for this.

The majority of this book was written in the place often regarded as *Iolkos* where the Greek myth places the home of Jason and where the *Argo* set sail in search of the Golden Fleece. This was an appropriate setting to collect my thoughts, particularly aided by early morning walks on the harbour front to witness the arrival of the fishing fleet and the sale of the catch of the day. Thanks to the staff of the University of Thessaly Library for their assistance and especially to Dr Elisabeth Kirtsolglou and the Kirtsolglou family, Lita and the late Danos, who made the stay in Volos both possible and pleasurable.

A number of colleagues have read all or part of the manuscript and I would like to thank Andrew Fleming, Jonathan Wooding and Paul Wallin for their incisive comments and help with improvement.

I dedicate this book to Sarah Daligan and Cerys Rainbird, who have had to tolerate my desire to complete it. I would like to register my heartfelt thanks to them both for their patience and love in the knowledge that it would not have been possible without them.

Lampeter, February 2007

A Consciousness of the Earth and Ocean

The Creation of Islands

The geographical study of islands is the study of movement. In their creation, islands may have drifted as pieces of land separated from their continental birthplace. Water may have invaded the once-dry valleys which had previously joined the current island to larger pieces of land. Oceanic islands may have moved rapidly from the ocean floor to emerge above sea level or, as they sink, through the organic growth of coral, the island may be transformed as coral and trapped detritus struggle to maintain a breach in the surface of the water. According to Gilles Deleuze (2004: 11), the movement embodied in islands is the 'consciousness of the earth and ocean', a place where the dual elements of the earth's surface are in sharp relief. Oceanic islands would be mountains if not for water; the wet and the dry cannot be separated, but the unstableness of these conditions is often on display.

According to Deleuze, the movement of islands makes them good to think with. They help provide conceptual spaces both for new beginnings and detachment. Additionally, islands are timeless as they are always on the move. Deleuze finds that 'islands are either from before or after humankind' (2004: 9). However, this is not an arbitrary space; it is constructed space, a space dreamt of and mythologized. For Deleuze, it is when we no longer understand these myths that literature begins, as it is an attempt to 'interpret, in an ingenious way, the myths we no longer understand, at the moment we no longer understand them, since we no longer know how to dream them or reproduce them' (2004: 12).

This book is an attempt to expose the myths and interrogate the dreams by which the study of islands in archaeology is often achieved. Such studies are occasionally grouped under the terms of a proposed sub-discipline of archaeology, 'island archaeology'. As we shall see, the study of islands as a unit of analyses in archaeology developed as a product of the 'new' or 'processual' archaeology in the 1970s, at which time quantitative techniques suited the supposed clear parameters provided by island space. In the 1980s, such approaches were critiqued and fell out of favour, and although it did not disappear completely, island archaeology also succumbed to this change. In recent years, island archaeology and island studies generally have come back to the fore and a contemporary topic of archaeology is the debate as to the utility of island archaeology for understanding the archaeological history of these places. The simple question is: Is there anything special about the archaeology of islands that requires a specific set of methodological and interpretational techniques different from that found on continents?

My intention is to show that, in part, the answer is a qualified 'yes', but for the most part it is a 'no'. It is mostly negative because I believe that we have been asking the wrong question and therefore debating the wrong issues. There can be no doubt, as I will show, that the Western imagination has placed islands as a special category of space in which to create myths and dreams, whether the sand

and palm trees stand for a relaxed holiday haven or an isolated slow death as a marooned castaway. As such, we have to treat islands in a particular way, not only to recognise these biases, but also to interrogate how this distinction came about. In this latter exploration, it is another environmental factor which I wish to highlight, that of the sea. Islands are defined by their being pieces of land surrounded by water, and this encircling creates the condition of insularity.

In this book, my interest lies in seawater and I do not consider islands in freshwater lakes, or indeed inland seas, as I wish to develop a thesis that links islands to the maritime environment. Indeed such an approach, one which decentres the land as the key defining geographical element, allows the development of an archaeology of islands that has at its heart a requirement to conceptualise coastal peoples, whether living on an island, boat or continent as members of maritime societies. This is the goal of the book that was not clear when I started the writing process. In debating the role of islands in archaeological understandings of the past, I have often been struck by the implicit or explicit expectation that islands equal isolation and this has formed the basis of much of my critique of island archaeology. However, while working through this book it has become clear that islands form only a part of a much more complex story, the story of maritime communities. Viewing islands in relation to maritime communities takes the book in the direction of an archaeology of the sea and begins to attempt to locate a different narrative, one still including but less dependent on bounded islands. To achieve this viewpoint, we need to go through the history of island studies to develop some key case studies. Therefore, this book in total represents only a point in a journey with a variable wind slowly pushing my intellectual pursuits into uncharted territory.

In this and the next two chapters, I will attempt to unpack the myths of islands and turn first to ecclesiastical history and then to popular literature as indicators of the perception of islands and the concept of island as, primarily, a metaphor for isolation.

▦ 'FULL FATHOM FIVE': ISLANDS IN WESTERN HISTORY

According to John Gillis (2003), before the fifteenth or sixteenth century, the concept of an island in the Western hemisphere was normally associated with land-locked places such as the *insulae* of residential blocks and neighbourhoods. This, of course, harked back to a classical tradition, as did the conceptualisation of the world as formed by the land of three continents, Africa, Asia and Europe. The land formed by the three continents, *Orbis Terrarum*, was surrounded by water, creating in effect an island of all the land. But it is clear from classical sources that islands were known off the edge of Europe, one of which was given the name of Cassiterides by Strabo in acknowledgment of it being an extremely important source of tin (Cunliffe 2001). However, islands appear to have been sought for specific purposes among the adherents to the new Christian Church which was becoming established during the end of the Roman Empire in the West.

The early Christian mentalité, closely aligned with the long-held pagan beliefs of the natives, found powerful magico-religious associations with places on the fringe of the Christian world. In a number of publications Tom O'Loughlin (1997, 1999, 2000) has explored the attraction of the islands on the fringe of the world known to early Christianity. O'Loughlin makes a distinction between the known seas of the Mediterranean, where known islands were located, and the sea surrounding the continents, which was the *Oceanus*, a threatening place where the tides mimicked the breathing of a living animal, possibly the primeval 'abyss'. The ocean could be full of demons, making it not unlike the desert spaces of the known world. Monks and hermits were attracted to these places as it was seen as their duty to do battle with the demons. An earlier use of deserts for this purpose appears to have been translated to the Ocean in the West. So the ocean as a metaphorical desert hangs strongly in allusions to the monastic heritage of ascetic isolation derived from the Egyptian desert, the inversion of the island/land and sea/water dichotomy is found in the oasis/water and desert/land model, with water and sand providing the conditions for otherness and evil.

The unknown spaces of the ocean also provided mappers of the world with conceptual spaces in to which they could place known but unlocated places. So, for example, the Garden of Eden was located on an island in the *Oceanus*, as were other 'promised lands'. According to O'Loughlin (1999), this is part of the point of the allegorical tale provided by the voyage of St. Brendan, who on a seven-year voyage battles demons and finds marvellous islands. At this date, in the early mediaeval period of western Europe, it is clear that islands and headlands on the larger islands of the Atlantic Archipelago were sought in 'pursuit of a desert' (Dumville 2002). In considering the community of monks residing in the monastery on Iona, located across a narrow sound from the Ross of Mull, in the Inner Hebrides of Scotland, O'Loughlin (1997) notes that they had found their desert fastness, as imagined. O'Loughlin also finds in *Vita Columbae* (The Life of St Columba) that the monastery was spread over a number of islands, that boat trips were regularly taken between them and indeed much further asea, with crafts going to and arriving from the mainland, Skye, the Orkney Islands (*Orcades*), Ireland and France.

So although Horn, White Marshall and Rourke (1990: 3) find that 'it is among the stone ruins left on the Atlantic islands by small colonists of Irish monks that we find the boldest parallels to early Egyptian monasticism in Europe', it is also the case that the established monasteries on such islands were connected to distant places, ultimately to Rome and Jerusalem. However, the archaeological evidence does indicate that some may have achieved the ascetic ideal. Perhaps the most spectacular example of this is the long-unrecognised hermitage on the South Peak of Skellig Michael, off the Atlantic coast of County Kerry, Ireland, the remains of which were located on an artificial platform over 200 metres above sea level. The island is also home to a remarkable mediaeval monastery constructed of corbelled stone beehive structures (Horn, White Marshall and Rourke 1990).

Clearly then, for a thousand years prior to the fifteenth century, islands were regarded as suitable locations for ascetics in monasteries and hermitages. Of course, metaphorical deserts were also provided by forests, deep valleys and mountain peaks. Islands then did not have a monopoly on use for this purpose, but the ocean as a mysterious and unknown place retained its power as a place to fire the imagination, as can be seen from the literature that grew up in the wake of this conceptualisation.

■ SUFFERING A SEACHANGE: ISLANDS IN POPULAR LITERATURE

We have already seen how some islands were imagined as 'promised lands' in the mediaeval mind, so it is no surprise that Thomas More's *Utopia*, published in 1515, is set on an island. The location chosen for this fictional society is a peninsula which King Utopus purposefully separates from the mainland by having a channel constructed across the isthmus so the sea could flow on all sides. As a literary device, this would have provided the contemporary reader with the clear message that this was a place of imagination where political dreams could be explored outside of reality. At this time, distant islands in the *Oceanus*, the Atlantic, were coming within the ambit of Europe for the first time. Between AD 1420 and 1472 the Madeiras, Azores, Sao Tome and Cape Verde islands had all been (re)discovered by Portuguese mariners looking for promised lands and the 'Fortunate Isles' (Gillis 2003; Mitchell 2004). The Canaries were settled many centuries prior to this, perhaps more than 2000 years ago, by people from the African coast lying 90 kilometres to the east (Mitchell 2004). Gillis (2003: 23) reports that in 1492 Christopher Columbus, in searching for the route to East Asia, made terra firma in the Caribbean. 'True to this mythical geography, Columbus's first landfall was an island. Everything he encountered was interpreted analogically in terms of the legendary isles that filled his mental maps.'

If Thomas More was aware of these discoveries while writing *Utopia*, then most likely he would have regarded them in relation to prophecies of finding Eden as an island out there. Each time Eden was not found, the search was on for another one. As Gillis (2003: 25) continues: '[T]he myth of Eden, like that of other legendary isles, was kept alive by the process of discovery itself, with Eden always located just one step beyond the moving frontier.'

Such motivations, of finding promised lands and untold riches, finally drew the British into maritime explorations, so that by the time William Shakespeare was writing his 1611 play *The Tempest*, Sir Francis Drake had circumnavigated the globe. Tales of adventures and perils on the high seas and the people, animals and places encountered on the way would have been circulating in London society. In this context it is unsurprising that Shakespeare locates *The Tempest* on an imaginary island. Although it is an island rather closer to home in the Mediterranean, such closeness is diminished by its island status, and a magical netherworld is created. That Shakespeare had stories of islands elsewhere in mind is occasionally suggested by the naming of the main protagonist's servant-creature Caliban, perhaps a dimly understood reference to the Carib people of the Caribbean. As Gillis (2003: 24) makes clear:

> From the start, Europeans held highly ambivalent, unstable views of the peoples they encountered in the Caribbean and the mainland of the Americas. Sometimes they were treated as nonhuman cannibals and monsters, but just as often they were assimilated to the image of simple nobility that Europeans attributed to their own pagan past.

Shakespeare may have been picking up on one of these views and playing with the likely acceptable notion that islands are strange places where strange things happen. Cyprian Broodbank (1999a) has pointed out, however, that in *King Richard II* Shakespeare recognises that he too lives on an island, in pointing to 'this sceptred isle', but the kingdom of England was not in reality an island and the allusion to island is likely to be as a metaphor for boundedness (John of Gaunt, the protagonist, goes on to say 'England, bound in with the triumphant sea'). At the time of writing in 1595, only seven years had passed since the Spanish Armada had been defeated as much by a stormy sea as the lawn-bowl-relaxed tactics of Sir Francis Drake. The sea and the realm must have been strongly to the fore in imagination during this period.

Shakespeare's island is a strange, otherworldly place that suffers most from its desolate condition. Moving a century ahead, the solitary island of Shakespeare and the solitary human are brought together in probably the most famous of island books. Daniel Defoe's *The Life and Strange Surprising Adventures of Robinson Crusoe, of York, Mariner* was published in 1719, and in recent times it has been generally accepted to be based on the experiences of Alexander Selkirk, who was marooned on the Juan Fernandez Islands in the South Pacific Ocean. Once again the fortunate isles are replaced with a sense of purgatory in isolation. Crusoe believes he deserves this purgatory, and his emotional journey can perhaps be compared with the penitential voyages on the *Oceanus* of the early Christian period (cf. Wooding 2001). Crusoe's 'Island of Despair' was empty of other humans apart from those of his nightmarish imaginings, and when humans did finally come ashore, he was wise to be wary, as they were cannibals.

The themes of isolation on islands and a fear of the unknown found in *Robinson Crusoe* continue in the nineteenth century and are exemplified in the works of such notable authors as Robert Louis Stevenson and Thomas Hardy. The main protagonist, David Balfour, in Stevenson's 1886 *Kidnapped* is thrown overboard from a ship in a storm and washed up on what he believes to be a small island in the Inner Hebrides of Scotland. Like Crusoe, rather than hoping to find inhabitants to aid his rescue, Balfour is fearful of not being alone. Eventually he is noticed by a passing fishing boat and finds that he is only on a tidal island and could have walked to the nearest settlement. The fear of islands, or rather what he imagined they meant, had led to irrational behaviour and unnecessary trauma. However, Balfour does accept that someone with experience of a marine environment (a 'sea-bred boy') would not have made the same mistake.

Hardy's novel *The Well-Beloved*, published as a complete work in 1897, is set in London and the 'Isle of Slingers', Hardy's fictional name for Portland Bill. Portland Bill is located on the Dorset coast in southern England and is a peninsula connected to the mainland by a spectacular beach constructed of storm-tossed pebbles. Although known today as the Isle of Portland, it is not physically disconnected from the English coast. For Hardy the island ascription is key, and the 'characteristics of the islanders' take on a central importance in understanding the narrative. The story involves a 'native' of the isle, Jocelyn Pierston, who has been able to spend many years away in London as an artist mixing in high society. Hardy emphasises the juxtaposition between the polite London society of Pierston's most recent acquaintance and the simple isolated conservatism and in-breeding of the 'islanders'. Using the island-like attributes of the promontory of Portland Bill eased Hardy's desire to juxtapose city/rural, cosmopolitan/isolated, modern/antiquated, educated/simple. Through this polarisation, the 'natives' of the 'Isle of Slingers' became the anthropological 'other'.

Many similar examples can be drawn from modern literature (see Rainbird 1999a and Broodbank 1999a). In much writing of literary islands there appears to be a process, beginning with a perception of physical isolation, through mental isolation (having few people with whom to express these fears), on to introspection and finally imaginings which include nightmarish subjects.

As each utopia or promised land was discovered, mapped and exploited, the search began for the next one. The Americas were viewed very much from perceptions, and thus, expectations of the 'old world'. It took at least two centuries for Europeans to begin to understand that these were new continents consisting of many things that were previously completely unexpected (Gillis 2003; Pagden 1993). In the meantime, the searching continued and only six years after *Utopia* was published, Ferdinand Magellan found a passage at the southern tip of South America. Magellan entered an ocean new to European mariners and named it Pacific on account of the calm weather he encountered. In March 1521 Magellan made the first historically recorded European landing on a Pacific island; death and destruction of property were an immediate consequence for the islanders. In the following centuries the islands of the Pacific were regarded as the abode of strange people who were poorly known and exoticised either as 'cannibal monsters' or 'noble savages'. Accounts of Anson's 1742 sojourn on Tinian in the Mariana Islands provided Rousseau with fuel for his noble savage philosophy, but did not take into account that this garden island, a 'paradise' for Anson's expedition that had survived a difficult crossing of the Pacific, was only such because the Spanish had previously forcefully removed the indigenous population (Barratt 1988). Even by the late eighteenth century and the expeditions of Captain Cook, the people and fauna were still being poorly represented in image and text (Smith 1989, 1992). The temptations of the Tahitians and the treachery of the Hawaiians were simplistic devices for attempting to understand difference. However, this was a two-way process, as Margaret Jolly (1996: 203) reports: '[i]n many oral and written traditions authored by Hawaiians, venereal diseases are portrayed as the "curse of Cook".'

It is not surprising then that the islands of Oceania not only gave to Europe 'tattoos' and 'taboo', but also a vision of islands spread as tiny dots across a vast ocean where, in their apparent isolation, 'primitive' people enacted strange rites which, on occasion, included cannibalism (McGrane 1989). As the Enlightenment saw the known world expand and distance become compressed, at least from a European perspective (Harvey 1990), the encounters being reported changed the way European people viewed themselves in the world. Part of the changing perception of the world was of islands, which rather than being considered ideal locations for a perfect society, to a certain extent insulated from other political regimes, were now considered dangerous in their isolation and for their perceived propensity to produce strange forms of human life. This perception has developed over a period of some 500 years and the myth of 'insularity = isolation' has been a popular way of writing about islands for popular consumption in the West. In the next section, I wish briefly to consider further the role of imaginary islands before considering some other typical uses of islands which have also contributed to use of islands as a metaphor for isolation.

IMAGINARY ISLANDS

We have already seen that in the mediaeval West, islands were mapped as biblical or imagined spaces in the *Oceanus*. These imagined islands were located on the periphery or even beyond the known world. These places had to be somewhere, but exactly where was not known. Even after Europeans began to find Atlantic islands, their locations altered on the map because of the inability to establish longitude, and also perhaps to reduce the chances of other mariners locating them because the islands became valued possessions. However, other completely imagined islands remained on the charts. In the Atlantic an enduring imagined island was Brasil, supposedly situated west of Ireland. Brasil (Brazile), perhaps named after the Gaelic dynasty of Uí Bre(a)sail, according to Dumville (2002) apparently held an inexplicable fascination for voyagers in the fifteenth and sixteenth centuries. Searching for Brasil possibly came to stand for voyages of discovery, and Brasil could be any yet unrecorded land. Carl Sauer (1968) believes a record of a voyage from Bristol, England in 1481 may well have been a cover for a fishing trip to Newfoundland, given the amount of salt they had taken on board.

In Oceania, origin stories from various eastern Polynesian islands relate to a homeland island of Hawaiki. In western Polynesia origin stories tell of the homeland island of Pulotu (Kirch and Green 2001). Although attempts have been made to identify actual islands with these ancestral places, it is difficult to identify any single actual islands to fulfil these roles. Perhaps more interesting, Polynesian islanders imagine their ultimate ancestral homelands as being islands rather than continents.

▪ ISLANDS OF THE DEAD

Gillis (2003: 26) finds that during Occident's Age of Discovery:

> For 300 years, islands were to be the refuge, not only of
> Europe's most compelling dreams, but also of its greatest
> nightmares. In European minds islands were the resorts of
> cannibals, monsters, demons, and witches, visions which
> were no longer allowed to range within Europe itself but
> now took up residence on Europe's new frontiers, always
> just sufficiently removed to be credible.

Such a degree of separation may also be why islands have often
been associated with the dead. The space provided by water acts
as a social separation between the living and the dead. Tony Pollard
(1999) explored the theme islands of the dead in relation to Scotland,
finding that the history of this association may be as old as the islands
and their first inhabitants in the Mesolithic (see Chapter 7), but con-
centrating on mediaeval and modern examples. In these examples,
he finds the distribution of graveyards, which are often associated
with small churches or chapels, is coastal, but more specifically on
places where clear views of the sea are available such as promontories,
high clifftops and prominent knolls. In addition to these locations,
burial grounds are found on islands in sea and freshwater lochs, indicating for Pollard that a deliberate policy was to use these locations
to isolate the dead from the living. Pollard noted in passing that
in the past in Ireland all of the souls of the dead were thought to
assemble at 'Tech Duinn' meaning 'House of Don', three islands
in Ballinskelligs Bay on the County Kerry coast. The fact that the
Scottish examples are located away from settlements indicates that
the burial rites must have incorporated an element of travel, perhaps
procession, in transporting the corpse from place of death to grave.
The crossing of water in such rites in order to access the other world
of the dead is referred to in classical literature onwards, and dating
from earlier times in Egypt, where a ship transported the dead. The

notional ferry man plays an important role in transporting the dead, and grave goods may be offered to pay for the service. Travel and voyage are both, of course, metaphors for individual lives, with a beginning, middle and end. Equally though, the water in a funeral rite has the potential to represent a liminal zone, a place in between life and death. I will return to this in the following section.

Colin Richards (1996) notes that in virtually all non-Western cosmological schemes, water provides a potent metaphor for thinking about and describing transition and transformation. The metaphors of travel and the role of water in achieving this and separating the worlds of the living and the dead are, as we shall see in this book, often invoked for the interpretation of the funerary and associated archaeology on islands. It is worth pointing out here that Pollard (1999: 34) also notes that cemeteries anywhere in the Highlands of Scotland have 'bastion-like walls isolating the domain of the dead within from that of the living without.' That is, if clear boundaries are required, then humans are able to manufacture them.

Although not indicating an antiquity as old as that suggested by Pollard for islands of the dead, the fascination of islands for early religious communities to found hermitages and monasteries may also have appealed to the dead as well as the living. Charles Thomas's excavations on the island of Lundy, located in the Bristol Channel, revealed a burial ground of this date. Lundy is a granite plateau 5 kilometres long and 0.8 kilometres wide, rising to a height of 140 metres, and being surrounded by steep cliffs with only one landing place (Figure 1). Nineteen kilometres from the north Devon coast at Hartland, Lundy is visible on clear days from locations in Wales and England. It appears that Lundy was settled, or at the very least regularly used, prior to this in prehistory as is attested by stray finds of stone tools and field systems with associated round houses. Thomas (1994) finds that on Beacon Hill, the highest point of the island, an early Christian cemetery was founded on the remains of a Romano-British farmstead. The farmstead contained ceramic vessels known as *briquetage* used for extracting salt from seawater through evaporation, but the house was abandoned at the time the

1. Landing place, Lundy, Bristol Channel, UK (source author, 2003)

first burial took place in the fifth century AD. Thomas argues, from the pattern of the placing of later graves and the later still evidence of the removal of the bones from the focal grave, that this was the place of interment for Saint Nectan, or prior to this beatification, King Brychan of south Wales who abdicated knowing that his life was near an end and journeyed to Lundy to spend his final days at a fledgling religious community where he was eventually buried. That eminent people desired burial in island places at this time is also indicated by the folklore attached to Bardsey Island/Ynys Enlli, an island with a distinctive high hill located in the Irish Sea a short crossing from the tip of the Lleyn Peninsula in north Wales. Here, according to the medieval *Vitae of Elgar and Dyfrig*, is the resting place of 20,000 saints (Jonathan Wooding, pers. comm.).

As indicated by the quote at the beginning of this section, islands have also been associated with malevolent beings, such as witches and demons, and the Bahamas were first recorded in 1503 by the Spanish as the Isle of Devils (Gillis 2003). Christer Westerdahl (2005) notes that the Baltic Sea island of Blåkulla (or Blå Jungfrum, meaning Blue Virgin or Blue Mermaid) is known across the North as a meeting place for witches. First recorded in the sixteenth century, sacrifices were made here to appease the Mermaid (or the Virgin) and avert the threat of bad weather. On the island is a large stone maze, which is supposed to be an instrument of magic in relation to fishing – a similar undated maze can be found at Troytown on the island of St Agnes in the Isles of Scilly, off the southwest coast of Britain.

PRISON AND PLANTATION ISLANDS

As far as one can get from the idealised image of the holiday island (however, that may be conceived in the imagination of the individual) are the prison and plantation populations of islanders held against their will. As places where malevolent spirits and people reside, islands must have offered an obvious location, along with their apparent boundedness, for the incarceration of people regarded as undesirable elements of society. Alcatraz in San Francisco Bay, California, and Robben Island in Cape Town Bay, South Africa, both have their origins in the settler societies that colonised the neighbouring mainlands. Both are now defunct and can be visited as part of a tourist itinerary, and in each are found opportunities to raise awareness of past injustices meted out to the colonised indigenous people of the area. Another, similar example is the former prison of Sarah Island in Macquarie Harbour in western Tasmania. Sarah Island had a much shorter history as a prison (1822–1833) than either Alcatraz or Robben Island, but has gained notoriety through the fictional writing of Marcus Clarke in his 1874 *For the Term of His Natural Life*, and perpetuated in the tales of horror and cannibalism linked to punishment and attempts to escape in the surrounding dense rainforest. Visitors to Sarah Island experience the passage of Clarke's protagonist Rufus Dawes by boat from the Southern Ocean through 'Hell's Gates' at the entrance to Macquarie Harbour before penetrating deep into the estuary for a National Park Service tour of the island. Returning to the boat, the tour then winds its way up part of the Gordon River where the 'natural' wilderness of the temperate rainforest can be enjoyed. As has been pointed out by Richard Flanagan (1996), the indigenous people and the convicts assigned the task of chopping timber here are not a feature of the commentary.

Tasmania, an island in itself, has another notorious historic penal institution at Port Arthur. Here the institution's burial ground was located on a small offshore island known today as the 'Isle of the Dead'.

Yannis Hamilakis (2002) provides a different example of the prison island. The island in question is Makronisos, located in sight of Attica near Athens, Greece. Today it is under the protection of the Ministry of Culture and described as an uninhabited bare island 13.5 kilometres in length and 1.5 kilometres wide. However, beginning in the Greek Civil War, from 1947 to 1950 it was the enforced home of 40,000 to 50,000 people. The majority of these were regarded by the authorities as left-wing sympathisers who were sent to a series of camps on the island for re-education prior to becoming conscripts of the nationalist forces. Re-education involved hard labour, torture, occasional isolation and ideological training by means of preparing propaganda and listening to speeches from prominent visitors. The labour included constructing the buildings for the camps including residences for the military commanders, cookhouses and churches, but related to ideological training they also were required to construct open-air theatres in the ancient Greek style and replicas of various other monuments from classical antiquity. These monuments included the Erechtheion, Temple of Athena and Parthenon, all features of the Acropolis in Athens. The island was given the ironic name the 'New Parthenon' by the inmates, for whom these monuments and heritage became key symbols in attempts at nationalist indoctrination.

For our purposes, it is particularly interesting to note that Hamilakis opines that an island may have been chosen for its bounded 'laboratory'-like status suitable for experimentation. In particular he draws on the work of French philosopher Michel Foucault in identifying that Makronisos in its schools, hospitals, theatres and other attributes typical of communities elsewhere was an 'enacted utopia', a heterotopia, an attempt to create the perfect space where entrance and exit were strictly controlled and inhabitation was designed for re-education.

Although prison and plantation islands are usually regarded as apparently chosen for their defined and controllable spaces and divisibility from urban centres, Gillis (2003: 29) takes the view that in contrast to being peripheral and isolated, actually:

> For most of the Early Modern period, islands afforded strategic advantages that no landlocked outposts could offer. They, not mainlands, were the initial points of trade on the African and American coasts. Without a dynamic sea of islands offering psychological security as well as material support for the triangular trade that was at the heart of commercial capitalism, it is hard to see how the slave trade and the plantation economies it made possible could have flourished.

The islands of the Atlantic were there to be exploited and initially they were stripped of anything of value, which was replaced by the importation of European animals and crops. 'Islands suited the dreams of imperial control particularly well . . .' (Gillis 2003: 26), as they could be possessed, colonized and the people dominated by force.

Islands as entrepôts were found off the east African coast, too. For example, by 1200 years ago, Muslim traders had established settlements on islands off the east coast of Africa. The Arabs became the mediators of trade contact between the Africans and Chinese (Dathorne 1996). Mitchell (2004), in reviewing the African islands, finds that the earliest evidence for such a role may come from Pemba. Located on coastal islands, such settlements for trade, exchange and opportunities to exploit mainland resources may be perceived by mainland communities as less threatening than an actual presence on the mainland and within one's own territory. These places may also be more inviting for overseas traders who could view the island as commercial rather than national space. In the Americas, Manhattan may have played such a role, and recent history has shown how Hong Kong emerged from such a situation. Equally, the liminal zone provided by the beach, which has been a focus of the work of historical anthropologist Greg Dening (1980, 1992, 1996) in researching contacts between Pacific islanders and Europeans, may also provide a neutral space for exchanges. In early mediaeval western Europe it has been proposed that promontories and sand bars appear to have been suitable locations for entrepôts, often located in positions that provided easy access to inland waterways (Hodges 1982).

◼ INSIDERS AND OUTSIDERS

A common perception of islanders, particularly when viewed by outsiders, is that of shyness, unwillingness to communicate, inward-looking, conservative and traditional. Islands appear to be repositories of lost time, that is, places outside of time where the future has been delayed, where the stream of modernity has passed by with few opportunities to make land and influence the native practices. In part, this is why islands can be the home of malevolent beings, as discussed above. Islands are places where oral history and folklore hang strong on the harbour side. As we shall see, this was an attraction to anthropologists in the early stages of the development of that discipline, and it also with good reason that islanders may wish to be wary of new people or developments. For the most part, it is not because they sit outside of history that islanders are often considered wary, inward-looking and suspicious of strangers. Rather, it is the very fact that they have largely been in the mainstream of history that islanders understand only too well the consequences of openness to communication provided by the sea. For example, although in orthodox models the people of Easter Island self-destructed due to their isolation, the consequences of contact with Europeans saw their population devastated by violence, slave taking and disease (Peiser 2005; Rainbird 2002a). Although this is an extreme case, such consequences of European contact were not atypical of the experience of islanders across Oceania, leading many years ago to Alan Moorehead (1966) describing it as a 'fatal impact'.

Jacqueline Waldren (2002: 5) says of her ethnographic work on the Mediterranean Balearic island of Majorca that many islanders:

> explained their reticence to mix with outsiders to the fact that their history was one of drawing inward to avoid the many threats that continuously arrived from 'outside'. Insecurity was a keynote of island life in the past, both in terms of agriculture and subsistence as well as invasions, conquests and sackings by Moors, Arago-Catalan expansion [from the mainland], pirates or bandits. Today this insecurity concerns loss of identity and island values with the onslaught of foreign investment in extensive areas of the island.

Archaeological evidence for such insecurity may be observable. Andrew Fleming (2005) describes the hiding places hidden amongst the rocky scree slopes on the hillsides of St Kilda in the Atlantic. From these hollows, approaching craft could be assessed as to whether they contained a likely friend or foe and appropriate action taken depending on the assessment. That this was a potentially serious matter is indicated from the first historically recorded incident which concerned the visit of pirates in 1615. Fleming notes, however, that day or night it was not possible to step unannounced ashore on Hirta, the main inhabited island of St Kilda, as the dogs would provide a rousing welcome in their barking.

However, we need to be particularly careful with islands that we do not always treat the area of the island and that of the human population as one community. This conception, a product of boundedness, is, as we shall see, key to biogeography, but is at odds with human social uses of such places.

SHORES AND LINES ON A MAP – BOUNDARIES AND SCALE

As we have seen, geographers from Strabo to mediaeval times often represented the land of the known world as surrounded by sea, with odder and stranger people, fauna and flora further from the centre and closer to the fringes being illustrated (O'Loughlin 1997; Ray 2003). Here we could invoke a distance/knowledge ratio, in that the greater the distance from home, the less the knowledge of the place, which equals a greater requirement to fill the gaps in knowledge with imagination. Home is usually the centre of the world; cognitive mapping begins there, whether that home is sedentary or mobile, a single structure or a territory, 'my country' as indigenous Australians refer to home. In the present day, however, with our familiarity of the view of Earth from space, and it is sobering to remember that only two generations have grown up with this image, it is easier to conceptualise the planet as home and the aliens as coming from another planet, rather than from over the horizon.

All of the land on Earth, as can be seen from orbiting spacecraft, is surrounded by water, whether liquid or frozen on the surface. As such, the geographical definition of an island would mean that all dry land was a suitable area of study for island archaeology. However, by geographical definition, the continents are not islands; hence Africa, Asia, Europe, North America, South America and Antarctica are not defined as islands. Australia, land and nation surrounded by seawater, or 'girt by sea' according to the national anthem, is in current orthodoxy too large to be an island and is defined as a continent. The claim for the largest island is usually given to Greenland (2,175,600 km^2), although much of this is permanently bound by ice to continental areas within the Arctic Circle, followed by New Guinea (790,000 km^2), Borneo (743,000 km^2) and Madagascar (588,000 km^2). These are large islands indeed, and it has been questioned whether large islands warrant the attention of a specifically island studies approach (cf. Parker Pearson 2004).

Island archaeology tends to be regarded as a combination of smallness and remoteness. That is, an island can be a small island anywhere, unless they are too close to the mainland as John Cherry (2004) has opined in regard to the islands of the Aegean Sea, or so distinctively geographically remote, or with a longevity of insularity, that their large size is counteracted, for example, the islands of

2. The end of an island? Bridge to the Isle of Skye under construction, Scotland, UK (source author, 1995)

Aotearoa/New Zealand (two islands totalling 265,000 km^2) or Tasmania (60,600 km^2). This book, where islands are discussed specifically, is for the most part concerned with smaller islands, or smaller islands in an archipelago including larger islands (e.g., Chapter 7; Britain 219,000 km^2 and Ireland 84,400 km^2); but as will be described in the following chapters, land should not necessarily be our paramount concern and the issue of scale is relative. Archaeologists of islands can be selective in regard to whether or not they self-define as island archaeologists.

It is also the case that the boundedness of islands, and in Chapter 2 I will show this is required in relation to biological studies of flora and fauna in an island biogeographical approach, can easily be overemphasised when discussing human populations (Figure 2). It is the ideal concept of the island, the connotation of the island metaphor that Rosemary McKechnie (2002) finds requires 'clear boundaries', a 'clear outside and inside' allowing 'closure and manageable scale' where 'difficult concepts such as tradition/modernity; marginal/dominant; past/present can be constituted with a clarity, that boundaries don't have elsewhere' (McKechnie 2002: 131). But, as Jonathan Wooding (1996) has pointed out, in modern and medi-aeval times, the coast was not used for socio-political boundaries. In fact, socio-political boundaries do not run along the line where land meets sea, but are established at some distance away from the land and out to sea or across parts of the island. The coast of an island may not provide a clear boundary or even a shifting bound-ary. The liminal zone often regarded as being defined by the coast as described above, particularly in locations where the tide creates temporal distinctions between land and sea, may not be liminal at all, but completely incorporated within the conceptual territories of coastal residents. In Australia, where the contemporary political spotlight has been on indigenous land rights, the focus in recent years has shifted for some communities to making claims for tra-ditional ownership rights over areas of the shore and ocean (Sharp 1996; McNiven 2003).

Conversely, Margaret Jolly (2001) has pointed out that the larger islands often have inland populations for whom the sea is rarely, and occasionally never, a feature of their lives. Examples illustrating this point come from New Guinea, where Highlanders have been taken to the shore either to be shocked by what was perceived as a wall of water in front of them, or a continuation of the sky or over-whelmed by saltiness of the sea (salt being a highly prized product inland) (Connolly and Anderson 1989; Gell 1995). Island commu-nities often have stories of other people living inland. Even on much smaller islands than New Guinea, such as Pohnpei in Micronesia (330 km^2), tales are told of small, malevolent beings living in the inland forests and mountains and the much larger Indonesian island of Flores (14,300 km^2), where similar stories have perhaps been authenticated by excavations of remains of very small hominids given the classification of *Homo floresiensis* (Morwood et al. 2004). Bound-aries may also be drawn notionally and politically across islands, with people at one end of an island having closer connections with people on the opposite shore than with people at the other end or side of the same island. These areas have been called 'passage areas' (Siegel 1996, quoted in Curet 2004; see also Broodbank 2000).

The use of islands in a search for clarity of definition can only lead to a reification of the dreams and myths represented by islands. As Tamara Kohn (2002) effectively illustrates in relation to her anthropological work in the Inner Hebrides of Scotland, visitors look for easy assurances that their concept of islands and islanders is unchallenged and, indeed, reinforced. An example is provided by the fisherman mending his nets by the quay who is asked if he has lived on the island all of his life, and he answers that he has, providing the visitors with an apparently eternal scene of island life. It turns out that this particular fisherman, although born on the island, had travelled the world and until his retirement back to the island had lived in the mainland city of Glasgow. Kohn makes the important point that he was not lying to the tourists, and in this and another case she presents:

> 'Islander' status would never be challenged for these two men because of their birth on the island and the deep genealogical links they hold with the place. Many years spent elsewhere returns them to the island with only that much more to offer it. Islandness is not defined by insularity, but insularity is constructed out of dreams and imaginations. (2002: 42)

ISLANDS IN A WORLD OF PERCEPTIONS

Little if any of what has been discussed above can be regarded as exclusive to islands, for as we have seen with boundaries and burial grounds, saints can and were buried in continental situations and witches inhabit inland places. As Westerdahl (2005) points out, the equivalent to an Island of Witches is found far from the sea at Blocksberg in the Harz Mountains of Germany. Although the British government has returned to prison ships with one moored at Weymouth Harbour in Dorset, the overcrowding of prison hulks, as they were called, is regarded as a key factor in the settling of Australia as a penal colony in 1788. The most notorious of British prisons is probably

Dartmoor Prison, located on the high granite moor lands of south-west England. Dartmoor has a reputation for desolation and isolation, although this, as in the case of islands, is more imagined than real. Arthur Conan Doyle's setting at Dartmoor of the Sherlock Holmes mystery of *The Hound of the Baskervilles* has done much to evoke this. Indeed, an island example of the opposite might be provided by the mutineers of the *HMS Bounty*, who in 1789, successfully set up home on the uninhabited Pacific island of Pitcairn in an effort to evade the pursuing authorities. They purposefully destroyed the ship by fire and in effect marooned themselves, perceiving this as freedom rather than imprisonment. Descendants of the mutineers continue to live on the island today.

In the following two chapters I draw on a wide range of biogeographical, archaeological, historical and ethnographical material in order to introduce the historical, critical and interpretative background to the four case study chapters (4, 5, 6 and 7). My concern as a prehistoric archaeologist, another problematic label (and by which I do not mean that I am attempting to elucidate a time before history; rather I am attempting to write an archaeological history of periods before significant written historical documentation), is to develop a history of maritime communities in the prehistoric past, by which I hope to render new interpretative possibilities. Himanshu Prahba Ray (2003) notes that such attempts in the past have usually been limited to accounts of waterborne trade, which is normally identified in archaeology by the presence of exotic and high-status items, and in doing this has ignored the potential richness of the fishing and sailing communities whose everyday activities are historically varied and interesting on their own account.

The case studies are chosen for specific reasons. In the case of Malta, it is to provide a direct comparison with historical approaches, which as we will see has been at the centre of debates concerning the utility of island archaeology. The next comparison is drawn from the Pacific Ocean and provides the historical circumstances in an autobiographical sense for the perspective I develop in this book, as it is the geographical area in which I have conducted the majority of my field research. Chapter 6 develops a maritime prehistory for the island of Gotland and allows for the continuation of themes developed in the previous chapters. It was through happy circumstance that my interest in islands offered an opportunity for exchange teaching at Gotland's higher education institution in 1997, which has continued to allow intermittent visits and the development of the perspective presented here. The final case study takes us into the Atlantic Ocean and the archipelago comprised of Britain, Ireland and their satellite islands. My first serious experience of archaeological excavation was on the Isle of Skye in the Inner Hebrides and was followed a couple of years later by my attendance as a student on a Sheffield University excavation in the Outer Hebrides. Chapter 7 represents the development of a perspective on an archaeology of islands, emphasising maritime connections in an area where archaeologists working on the islands would only rarely define themselves as 'island archaeologists'.

In Chapter 8, I ask if we have discovered anything distinctive about the history of islands which makes them a useful category to study separately from other types of archaeology. But, first we need to step back a little and look at the history of the archaeology of islands.

2

Seas of Islands

Anthropology, Biogeography, Archaeology and Postcolonialism

In this chapter, I will present the intellectual heritage of island archaeology derived from anthropology and bio-geography and then move on to consider how the perspective of islanders themselves can help inform the archaeological study of islands. Through this exercise we are able to recognise the intellectual boundaries that can stifle the interpretation of island history and lead us to consider new ways of considering islands.

■ ISLANDS AND ANTHROPOLOGY

Charles Darwin's visit to the Galapágos Islands in 1835, aboard *HMS Beagle*, was to have a profound effect not only on evolutionary theory and natural history, but also on the development of the discipline of anthropology. The conclusion he drew from his observations was that animals and plants, long isolated from one another by being on an island, can evolve into new, separate species from what was originally a single species, what he called 'speciation in isolation'. Darwin wrote of the chaffinches he saw:

> When I see these Islands in sight of each other, and possessed of but a scanty stock of animals, tenanted by these birds, but slightly differing in structure and filling the same place in Nature, I must suspect they are only varieties. . . . If there is the slightest foundation for these remarks the Zoology of Archipelagos will be well worth examination; for such facts would undermine the stability of species. (from Darwin's notebook, quoted in MacArthur and Wilson 1967: 3)

The conclusion he drew helped establish the theory of evolution, for here was proof that plants and animals were not created and unchanging in their founding image, but if separated from one another in distinct breeding populations they would take divergent evolutionary paths. At the same time as Darwin, but working in the islands of Southeast Asia, Alfred Russell Wallace was drawing the same conclusion. For the study of biological evolution and natural history beginning in the mid-nineteenth century, islands became marked as the ideal setting for fieldwork expeditions. As Henrika Kuklick (1996) has found, it was in this milieu that Alfred Cort Haddon, a Cambridge zoologist, first organised an expedition to the Torres Strait islands, located in the shallow seas between the Cape York Peninsula of the Australian mainland and the huge island of New Guinea. Haddon's encounters with the islanders fuelled an enthusiasm for the study of humans, and in 1898 he returned as leader of the Cambridge Anthropological Expedition to the Torres Strait (Stocking 1987). On this expedition he was joined by W. H. R. Rivers and C. G. Seligman, who, like Haddon, went on to become founding figures of social anthropology. Haddon's training in zoology meant that natural history principles became applied to ethnographic fieldwork, which is such a distinctive facet of anthropology as a discipline. Kuklick (1996) finds that human societies were expected to behave in the same way as other living organisms, so that when 'isolated' on an island, they would evolve into distinctive types. This led to the understanding that where distinctive island societies had been colonised by Europeans, they were under threat of extinction. In these situations ethnographic fieldwork was of great urgency if a record of the island culture was to be maintained. Complaints that anthropologists treated island societies as if they had no history (e.g., Gillis 2003) can be explained by the natural history paradigm, in that the supposed isolation of islands meant for Darwin that islands enjoyed 'light natural selection' inasmuch as competition for space was minimised as each plant and animal had an established niche, leading to a state of equilibrium. This stasis in floral and faunal development was also extended to humans, leading to notions of islanders as conservative and traditional. Haddon considered the islanders to be 'backward' and 'savage' in comparison to continental peoples, particularly Europeans, who because they were in constant contact and competition, continued to evolve (Kuklick 1996: 616). It appears to be the case then that from anthropology's founding moment as a discipline based on ethnographic fieldwork, islands became a focus for those wishing to study 'fossil' societies where the 'ethnographic present' was easily projected into a past of unknown duration.

In reality, however, the direct link between Darwinian notions of islands related to natural selection and speciation did not survive even the Torres Strait expedition. It soon became clear to the members of the expedition that the idiosyncrasies of human societies were not adaptations due to natural selection, but islands nonetheless remained important. Kuklick (1996: 625) states that islands 'became cultural rather than physical space.' Expectations of finding evidence of societal speciation were replaced by the hope of finding pristine societies whose island existence had kept them isolated and unsullied by contacts with Europeans or other aliens.

The Cambridge School of Anthropology influenced the next generation of British-based social anthropologists who also conducted their research on islands. These included A. R. Radcliffe-Brown, who went to the Andaman Islands in the Indian Ocean, and Bronislaw Malinowski, who famously travelled to the Trobriand Islands located east of the New Guinea mainland. Although islands for them were perhaps more about the hope of identifying a closed social system, where the functions could be identified, as was dictated by the functionalist paradigm of the day, Malinowski (1922) still recorded his intellectual debt to Haddon, Rivers and Seligman in his introduction to *The Argonauts of the Western Pacific*.

Kuklick (1996) traces the diffusion of the 'island model' through anthropology, and as we shall see in relation to island biogeography, island communities did not have to live on actual islands. Cultural islands were deemed to exist in continental situations, such as that of the Nuer people of Africa in E. E. Evans-Pritchard's influential work. A similar natural history heritage can be detected across the Atlantic, where practitioners of cultural anthropology in America were also attracted to island societies. This fact is not too surprising given that Franz Boas, the founder of the discipline, was originally trained as a geographer. A direct lineage can be traced back from Margaret Mead through her supervisor, Ruth Benedict, to Boas who had taught Benedict. Mead is another anthropologist famous in relation to the ethnographic fieldwork she conducted on islands. In New Guinea and Samoa, Mead saw her role as preserving the record of 'thousands of years of human history', betraying an adherence to the synchronic assumption of the ethnographic present, ahead of contact by missionaries, and introductions of guns, alcohol and disease. In a fine example of the application of the 'island model' she believed that unsullied peoples were only to be found 'isolated on small Pacific islands, in dense African jungles or Asiatic wastes . . .' (Mead 1942: 10–11).

As the limitations of functionalism became recognised, the island model was criticised and rejected in most anthropological circles (Kuklick 1996). Even so, in anthropology echoes of this earlier model can still be heard and Tamara Kohn (2002: 40) finds that recent island ethnographers, although they 'often celebrate the movement and change within and beyond island boundaries', do not always appear to recognise the need to fully unpack the traditions on which their work is based. Decolonisation in the post–World War II period, although still an ongoing project, has led to a critique of the purpose of anthropology in a connected world and the development of a more reflexive position in relation to the production of knowledge (e.g., Clifford and Marcus 1986; Clifford 1988). Such a critique has arrived late in the discipline of archaeology and, as I will argue below, the 'island model' retains some currency in archaeological discourse. Before discussing this, I first need to introduce the theory of island biogeography.

ISLANDS AND BIOGEOGRAPHY

The intellectual ancestry of the theory of island biogeography is explicitly in the findings of Charles Darwin in relation to the speciation in isolation introduced above. However, in their 1967 treatise, the proponents of the theory, MacArthur and Wilson, take the study of islands beyond that of evolutionary interest. They find that islands as objects of biogeographical study are appealing in being simpler than the complexity found amongst the flora and fauna in oceans and continents. The parameters of the study area are easy to set, being where the land meets the sea. The study area is easily labelled, it is the name of the island, and the population of plants and animals are easily labelled by the island of residence. They also find that the huge diversity of island forms and locations, having a wide range of shapes, sizes, ecologies and what they term 'degree of isolation', means they provide a series of 'natural experiments' which are ideal for the testing of hypotheses.

It is clear that islands continued to attract natural scientists for similar reasons to those expounded in the late nineteenth century, and the orthodox and necessary view of islands as insular and isolated is explicit in their approach. MacArthur and Wilson (1967) do accept, however, as in the 'island model' of anthropology, that to a certain extent, island-like habitats exist in continental situations. For example, where a group of trees is surrounded by grassland the trees become a habitat island, as the flora and fauna of woodland are distinct from that of grassland, so it is expected that the woodland population is isolated and unable to migrate across the grassland.

The aim of the authors was to develop quantitative theory for biogeography which could be used to test hypotheses. In order to achieve this, they had to establish variables. The 'area effect' is the size of the island; the effect of size is that a smaller island is expected to have fewer species of plants and animals in its population when compared to a larger island with greater space and more environmental niches. The 'distance effect' represents 'barriers to dispersal' in that the more distant from other land the island is situated, the more difficult it is for plants and animals to migrate to the island. In other words, the greater the distance of the water gap, the more effective a barrier to dispersal of plants and animals it becomes.

These two variables can be set up as an equation to provide an area/distance ratio, in which the variable of distance of island from continent is associated with land area of the island to provide an index of expected flora and fauna diversity on an island. It is expected in this model that a large island close to the mainland will have a greater number of species arriving and will be able to support more species than a small island distant from the mainland. The small distant island, although having fewer species arriving, is expected to exhibit more competition for space, leading to a further reduction in the number of species that the island can support. Any given island area would only be able to support a certain number of species. As long as an island was not 'closed' to a particular species due to 'packing' or to a resident competitor, then the newly arrived species would have to displace through extinction or extirpation an already resident species, leading to species equilibrium.

Another part of the theory, adopted from elsewhere, was the notion of the 'founder effect'. Founder effect occurs when a new species arrives on an island and, because of the small size of the founding group, the offspring inherit characteristics from a limited gene pool allowing for genetic divergence between the island population and that of the original mainland population. MacArthur and Wilson believed and demonstrated that aspects of the model could be tested in the bounded 'laboratory' of an island; for example, a new species could be introduced to an island and it could be observed as to whether the principles of species equilibrium operated.

Although E. O. Wilson is renowned for his views in support of the extremely deterministic view of human behaviour espoused in sociobiology, the theory of island biogeography was presented as a tool for understanding plant and non-human animal population dynamics. Several years after the publication of MacArthur and Wilson's treatise, however, archaeologists influenced by the 'new archaeology' were keen to adopt quantitative models from the natural sciences. The simple formulae provided by the theory of island biogeography was particularly attractive and, as we will see, has continued to be so, to archaeologists working in island settings, as a way of understanding island colonisation and the behaviour of islanders.

ARCHAEOLOGY AND ISLAND BIOGEOGRAPHY

John D. Evans, a long-term researcher in the Mediterranean, appears to have been the first to adopt island biogeography principles for archaeological purposes. In his 1973 paper, 'Islands as laboratories for the study of cultural process', in terms drawn directly from MacArthur and Wilson, he espouses the 'special' physical conditions of islands which made them particularly appropriate for the archaeological study of populations. He finds, as MacArthur and Wilson did, that the 'limitations' of islands in regards to their habitat provide 'significant advantages' and that '[t]hese qualities have been more fully recognized by natural scientists and anthropologists' (Evans 1973: 517). Of course, we have seen that this model had already been generally rejected in anthropology, and the natural sciences were interested in non-human populations, but Evans continued to set out a number if island attributes which have become influential in the archaeology of islands.

Evans finds (1973: 517–518) that the 'fundamental limitation' to islands is the sea which imposes restrictions, 'more or less', on the amount of contact possible with people elsewhere. This is, of course, the 'barrier effect'. A further positive attribute in Evans's mind was the light natural selection suffered by islands in that the isolation of their inhabitants 'whether plant, animal or human' removed them from the pressures of competition found on continents. The isolating barrier effect also meant that the inhabitants of islands were less likely to suffer significant ethnic and cultural change due to external imposition 'such as mass immigration or hostile invasion.' This is a fine example of the assumed conservative nature of islanders.

Because MacArthur and Wilson developed their theory of island biogeography for plants and non-human animals, Evans (1973) is required to add another attribute to his theory, 'locomotion', that is, the ability of humans to build and use sea craft. Such vessels involve various levels of sophistication, and Evans believed that the available technology in any given island context should be assessed.

The rare finds of remains of prehistoric sea craft mean that proxy indicators would need to be assessed to elucidate the technology available for crossing the 'barrier' provided by the sea. Once again, Evans finds that island contexts are particularly good for providing this information, due to the likely restricted range of local resources, that is, 'area effect'. In other words, objects derived from overseas will be 'relatively easy' to identify and from this 'we can build up a picture of the range of contacts available' (1973: 518). This, of course, is likely to be in relation to the 'area/distance ratio'.

Evans (1973), now going significantly beyond the theory of island biogeography, returns to the issue of isolation and the unique effects islands may have on human behaviour. He notes that there is a tendency for island societies to put inordinate amounts of effort into the construction of ceremonial and religious complexes, for

3. Hagar Qim, Malta. One of the Neolithic 'temples' constructed in monumental proportions using megalithic architecture (source author, 2000)

example, the 'temples' of Neolithic Malta (Figure 3) and the statues (*moai*) of Easter Island (Rapa Nui). He suggests that 'isolation and relative security (and perhaps boredom)' leads to a 'tendency towards *exaggerated development* of some aspect of their culture' (1973: 519, my emphasis).

In a later paper, Evans (1977) further developed his ideas in relation to Malta, but begins by conceding that in comparison with the islands of the Pacific Ocean, which are 'widely scattered specks of land in an enormous expanse of water', the isolation experienced by Mediterranean islands is only a 'relative one' (1977: 13). He finds that the Mediterranean islands serve best to illustrate interaction between islands and mainland and with other islands even if a 'degree of isolation is always present' (1977: 13). He then goes on to argue that during the temple building period on Malta, the island was 'closed' to outside influence, resulting in some sort of pressure developing in society due to lack of 'external stimuli'. This lack of external stimuli resulted in a necessary release of this pressure by the construction of monumental megalithic temples and rock-cut tombs; that is, there was a long process of *exaggerated development* of ritual which was expressed in *monumental elaboration.*

It is patently clear that it is not only islands where monumental elaboration has occurred. The megalithic tradition extends over much of western and northwestern Europe during the Neolithic and geographically includes both island and continent. Evans's bold statement cannot be accepted. Monumental architecture in the Americas, Egypt and other non-island locations demonstrates that such variety in cultural expression is by no means an exclusive outcome of island living. But more worrying is that this model, further developed in Evans (1977), continues to inspire archaeologists. The peculiarities of the island's archaeology mean that the Maltese example is particularly enduring (see Robb 2001).

Simon Stoddart and colleagues (1993) attempted to extend Evans's proposals. They find that islands, bounded and to a greater or lesser extent isolated, may give rise to the exclusive intensification (read, 'exaggerated development') of one aspect of power relations. For the Neolithic in Malta, they identify a cycle of 'monument-oriented' and 'exchange-oriented' societies that are a direct product of this island context. During the period of temple construction, they interpret the Neolithic societies of Malta as insular, a factor which evidently leads to the unique and elaborate monumental architecture that Evans had discussed. A temporally distinct cycle identified by the introduction of 'exotic' materials implies for the authors a shift to communication being re-established with the outside world and local power no longer derived from the monuments but through control over the exchange of exotic objects.

Another clear and deliberate use of island biogeography (in the guise of island 'sociogeography') can be seen in Mark Patton's 1996 book *Islands in Time*. Patton attempts to replace the emphasis on objects (i.e., monumental elaboration) with that of the subjects, finding that 'cultural elaboration' in the prehistoric societies of the Mediterranean islands is greatest on islands that are relatively large ('area effect') and furthest from the mainland ('distance effect'). The cultural elaboration is basically assessed by degree of monumental elaboration. The presence of monumental architecture on the Balearic Islands, Sardinia, Corsica, Malta and Crete is explained by this simple area/distance ratio correlation. How Sardinia (23,800 km^2), Corsica (8680 km^2) and Crete (8260 km^2) can be compared with relatively diminutive Malta (246 km^2), especially when we consider that Malta is in sight of Sicily (25,460 km^2), is not explained. This perhaps indicates Patton's struggle to add a social context to a model developed in the late 1960s and based on the nineteenth-century principles of the natural sciences. In this, the ancestral connections exhibited create a book-length treatise that in reality means the 'time' of the book's title may be considered that of the nineteenth century and the Darwinian biology of that period, rather than an investigation of the past peoples of the Mediterranean.

In Chapter 4, I look in detail at the issues raised here for Malta, and Mediterranean islands more generally. Evans's model went far beyond that envisaged by MacArthur and Wilson. In general the application of their theory to island archaeology has been more typically related to issues of island colonisation, with a basic assessment of the role of area and distance in the timing of human settlement on islands. Although implicit (and occasionally explicit) in these applications, humans can be regarded as behaving in ways typical of the fauna and flora studied by biogeographers.

John Cherry (1981) published a paper in which he made explicit that the model he was using had been developed for plants and animals, arguing that, 'Man, after all, is an animal and we *do* know something of the ways in which insularity affects the distribution and adaptation of animals' (1981: 64, emphasis in original). He used the distance and area equation as an aid to understanding the colonisation process of the Mediterranean islands and finds that based on the dates for first settlement available at that time, 'the order in which they were taken into use is to some extent simply a reflection of their size and their remoteness from the mainland' (1981: 58). Obviously, given the proviso 'to some extent', the opposite conclusion could have been drawn. In a later paper, Cherry (1990) replied to such criticisms by pointing out that he was being deliberately provocative and understood the limitations of such an approach.

Steve O. Held (1993) applied the island biogeography approach in an attempt to understand episodes of colonisation and cultural change on prehistoric Cyprus. Like Evans, he sees insularity as crucial. A measure of this for him is that Cyprus is rarely visible with the naked eye from the surrounding mainlands, and then only from the Taurus Mountains. In comparison to what was then known of the same period on the mainland, his interpretation was that isolation explained 'cultural retardation' and delayed the 'irreversible rise of social complexity by as much as 2000 years [until they] permitted themselves to be drawn into maritime interaction spheres [when] they gradually relinquished the secrecy and protection provided by their isolation' (Held 1993: 29). Although clearly loaded with evolutionary assumptions and no longer supported by the evidence (see note and references in Rainbird 1999a), Held's view, as we have seen, was one that is not atypical of perceptions of islands and islanders. Indeed, it is telling that in a conference abstract, Held (1990) said that islands were good for identifying the four processes of dispersal, survival, adaptation and extinction, with these linked to isolation and limitation being in Held's mind the two key attributes of islands.

William Keegan and Jared Diamond (1987) took island biogeography and considered its utility in relation to the colonisation of islands in a number of examples drawn from across the world. They found that the utility of the theory of island biogeography could be enhanced with the addition of the model of 'autocatalysis' in the relatively simple logic that once one island has been found in a particular direction, then it is likely, and prudent, to continue in that direction in exploring for other islands. In this model it will not necessarily be the nearest and largest islands that are settled first. Atholl Anderson (2003) has considered this a workable approach to modelling colonisation of the islands of Polynesia as has Cyprian Broodbank (1999b) for the Aegean islands. Keegan's research in the Caribbean makes such a model particularly understandable as the archipelagic chain of islands lend themselves very well to the autocatalysis model of colonisation.

Interestingly, L. Antonio Curet (2004) finds that approaches that may be regarded as specific to island archaeology have rarely been applied in the Caribbean context. He argues that this is in part due to geography, with the very close proximity of one island to another making notions of isolation and insularity hard to sustain, but also a tradition (as exemplified in the work of Irvine Rouse) in treating 'cultural units' as the bounded unit of analyses. In the Caribbean this rarely, if ever, equates to a single island, but rather single social groups are either distributed across a number of islands or, in the case of larger islands, may contain a number of distinct cultural units defined by material culture remains. With this in mind, it is interesting that biogeographical approaches are still attractive, and Keegan insists that 'islands *are* isolates and that human agency can only account for a relatively small subset of human behaviour' (1999: 255, emphasis in original). Atholl Anderson (2004) also points out that in the Pacific interpretations of 'Lapita people' and 'ancestral Polynesian society' have had similar effects to those described by Curet in creating cultural units which go beyond specific islands or archipelagos (see also Lape 2004 for Southeast Asian islands).

Marcy Rockman (2003) finds that biogeographical approaches to studies of colonisation have provided a popular alternative to culture change models of colonisation, including dispersal, migration and diffusion which fell out of favour, as previously discussed, when new quantitative methods were demanded for archaeological explanation. In recent years, outside of island archaeology, they have been most often applied for understanding gatherer-hunter dispersals in early prehistory, and appear to be an extension of previously popular optimal foraging models used to explain adaptation to the environment. As characterised by Rockman (2003), biogeographical models of human colonisation rely largely on the 'barrier effects' which are 'population barriers', 'social barriers' and 'knowledge barriers'. These barriers may totally preclude colonisation or act as filters as to what humans are able to transport across the barriers.

Peter Mitchell (2004), in a preliminary attempt to bring islands situated off the coast of Africa into the realms of island archaeology, applies aspects of island biogeography. Acknowledging that the islands of the Mediterranean are, geographically speaking, in the realms of his study area, he accepts that they have already been studied in such a way and concentrates on the islands located in the Red Sea, Indian Ocean and Atlantic Ocean. Application of distance and area against known date of colonisation highlights the late date of occupation of Madagascar, which with an area of 580,000 km^2 should according to the model have been settled much earlier than the current, albeit wide, estimates of 1000 to 2000 years ago. The accrued archaeological and linguistic evidence also points to the colonisation population as derived from Southeast Asia, which provides an example that makes a mockery of island biogeographical approaches where seafaring people are concerned, particularly those with an ability to transport a farming economy with which to adapt their new island home. As would be expected, Madagascar's ecology is altered by the colonists with evidence of clearance and the loss through extinction of several species of animals and birds, a common occurrence in the Mediterranean and the Pacific.

ISLANDS AND THE POSTCOLONIAL CRITIQUE

The work of Epeli Hau'ofa (1993) has resonated far beyond the already large world of Oceania at which it was directed. His reconceptualisation of the European-introduced concept of islands as isolated dots in a vast ocean, in to a localised perception of islands as joined in a 'sea of islands', has decentred the land and replaced it with the sea in the way people imagine island realms. Gillis (2003) talks of an Atlantic 'sea of islands' in the post-mediaeval period and Fleming (2005) references Hau'ofa as a source to aid understanding the Atlantic archipelago of St Kilda in regard to its inhabitants' relations to the wider world.

Hau'ofa, an indigenous islander trained as a social anthropologist (and now a successful novelist), recognised early on in his studies that there were problems with the ways that outsiders represented islanders. In a critical essay published in 1975, Hauʻofa set out the types of issues that were to become more widely broadcast in the publication of Edward Said's 1978 book *Orientalism*. His dissatisfaction with anthropological accounts of the time was expressed in a series of concerns:

> after decades of anthropological field research in Melanesia we have come up only with pictures of people who fight, compete, trade, pay bride-prices, engage in rituals, invent cargo-cults, copulate and sorcerise each other [there is no] literature to indicate whether these people have any such sentiments as love, kindness, consideration, altruism and so on. (Hauʻofa 1975: 286)

Hauʻofa emphasised the one-sided nature of colonial discourse, which is a theme he took up again in his influential 1993 paper, 'Our Sea of Islands'. In this paper he stated that he had found in fellow islanders a perception of their homes as small, poorly resourced and peripheral to the economic centres of the world. He identified this as the product of centuries of colonialism, where colonial administrators had imposed artificial boundaries across the sea to divide up territories for control and possession. Hauʻofa also believed that the teachings of the colonial governments emphasised that the homeland was centre and the islands the periphery. Even in decolonised contexts this continues due to the 'present condition of dependence on the largesse of wealthy nations' (1993: 4).

In contrast to conceiving inhabitation of islands as constricting and restricted to the land, Hauʻofa reminds the indigenous people of Oceania that:

> [t]he world of our ancestors was a large sea full of places to explore, to make their homes in, to breed generations of seafarers like themselves. People raised in this environment were at home with the sea. They played in it as soon as they

could walk steadily, they worked in it, and they fought on it. They developed great skills for navigating their waters, and the spirit to traverse even the few large gaps that separated their island groups. (1993: 8)

This passage evokes the 'sea of islands' as an oceanic world undivided by colonial interests. As we shall see, it is not without its problems, but in its efforts to focus on the sea as a means of communication and remove the perception of island life in the past as isolated and insular, it has much to recommend it and I will return to this in Chapter 3.

A paper by Thomas Eriksen (1993) provides an example of a reflexive anthropology which is more typical of social anthropology following the postcolonial critique. In it he asks, 'Do cultural islands exist?' Taking the Indian Ocean island of Mauritius as an example, he points to the fact that although located over 1000 kilometres from mainland Africa, the nearest continent, the island is home to a community derived from Africa, China, Europe and a variety of locations in the Indian sub-continent. Eriksen finds that deep continental valleys surrounded by mountains may indeed be more isolated from outside influence than even a geographically distinct island like Mauritius (Braudel 1972 also noted this for the Mediterranean). As an important aside, Madonna Moss (2004: 179) has said of the people who have inhabited the more than 1000 islands of the Alexander Archipelago in southeast Alaska for at least 10,000 years that 'the proximity of the islands to one another as well as their steep topography and dense vegetation comprised a world in which mountains and forest provided the boundaries between "islands" centred on saltwater passages and shorelines'.

However, the multiple origins of the Mauritians have resulted in ethnic differences that prompt Eriksen to consider using the term 'island' as a metaphor for the boundaries between these groups. Thus, the physical island does not inhibit external contact and promote isolation, but the islanders themselves actively promote distinctions and boundaries between ethnic groups. Indeed, any forms of isolation

41

found in Mauritius are the result of the people themselves forming exclusive communities. Eriksen concludes that even as metaphor the notion of island is not appropriate for discussions of society, as no society is ever truly isolated, and so 'island' could be replaced by 'peninsula', which would allow a clear boundary but with opportunities for contact across the isthmus.

■ SMALL WORLDS AND BIG ISSUES – MICROCOSMS

Despite the evidence derived from a more considered understanding of island communities, the notion of microcosm remains a popular trope amongst island archaeologists, and has most specifically been explored in relation to Easter Island/Rapa Nui (Bahn and Flenley 1992; see also Kirch 1997, Flenley and Bahn 2003). Microcosm suggests that an island can be a world in miniature apart from the actual world in which it exists. Like island biogeography, the establishment of the notion of microcosm requires the boundaries, parameters and edges to be clearly set and this for island archaeologists is where the land meets the sea. Within this boundary a notional little world functions without the need for contact with aliens beyond the bounds.

> Islands in their inherent isolation are highly individual worlds where their differences and similarities, both obvious and subtle, make them excellent places from which to observe the world, often in advance of world events. (frontispiece, Waldren and Ensenyat 2002)

So said the conference organisers of the 2001 World Islands in Prehistory conference in Majorca. For them the island as microcosm approach is clearly a distinct advantage. Also a product of the Majorca conference is a paper by Bill Ayres (2002), a long-term researcher of the archaeology of the Pacific islands, in which he provides a description of apparent sociopolitical centralisation on the island of Pohnpei in Micronesia. He states that it is appropriate to explore issues of social evolution here because islands as cultural and environmental 'laboratories' allow for long-term perspectives to be developed, and linked to this, compact environmental circumscription leads to rapid centralisation as there are limited locales for nucleation of settlement. In utilising these parameters Ayres claims that the case study of Pohnpei has illuminated:

> structural and processual change in *microcosm* [in which] the geographically *remote* Pacific islands provide striking illustrations of human imagination and creativity in prehistory. (2002: 66, emphases mine)

That 'imagination' and 'creativity' are there I have no doubt, but beginning a study of island societies with the microcosm as a model is, as we have seen, to perpetuate and reify the imaginations and dreams of Europeans. How can archaeologists approaching the study of islands avoid this narrowness of perception which may result in the archaeologist, to paraphrase Jones (1977), suffering a 'slow strangulation of the mind'?

A self-defined island archaeologist who has thought a great deal about this problem is Cyprian Broodbank. In his book, *An Island Archaeology of the Early Cyclades* published in 2000, amongst many other things, he has critically adopted some of the methods of island biogeography to provide a much rounder view of island living. He says that 'although island biogeography and island archaeology remain natural partners in investigating island worlds, the former cannot provide, and in fairness should not be expected to provide, an overall agenda for the history of islands' (2000: 363). Broodbank eschews the use of islands as individual units of analysis and his work takes an archipelagic approach in an attempt to understand the Neolithic and Early Bronze Age periods of the numerous islands making up the Cyclades group of islands in the Aegean Sea in the eastern Mediterranean. He recognises that as a group what is presented is a patchwork mosaic of land and sea and argues that '[w]e need an *archaeology of the sea* to match an archaeology of the land' (2000: 35). Broodbank also proposes that the bringing together of landscapes and seascapes gives us 'islandscapes' as a term which combines the patches of sea and pieces of land. Consequently, he says,

> island archaeology must seek to discern the forms of the ancient landscape . . . to practice an archaeology of the sea that is more than an archaeology of boats, to search for traces of sea-paths and modes of maritime interaction, movement and trade, and to engage with the detailed attributes and distribution of island material culture. (2000: 363)

So Broodbank is not proposing a maritime archaeology, but does incorporate the variables of maritime and marine technology, evidence for the exploitation of the sea and movement over it. Broodbank recognises the necessity and frequency of sea-crossings. In the study of islandscapes all this is added to the typical archaeology of island *terra firma*. In concluding his detailed application of this new approach to island archaeology, he identifies three themes which have emerged:

1. The alteration of islandscapes through time. That is, recognition that the boundaries are not always the same, which in the case of an archipelago makes for a 'fuzzy analytical set'. There is also no assurance that the archipelago was viewed in the past as a coherent group.
2. Movement, particularly by sea, is a constant. Things on the move include 'people, animals, foodstuffs, objects, materials, customs or ideas [with motives for movement ranging from] hunger to the pursuit of fame' (2000: 365).
3. The relationship between the archipelago and the outside world.

In all, Broodbank provides an admirable attempt to deal with the criticisms of island archaeology and take the archaeological study of islands on to another level of analyses and interpretation. This is a positive initiative in attempting to fully contextualise island living in the past, but I suggest it has a single and unavoidable fatal flaw: his commitment to islands themselves. Broodbank's ability to recognise island biogeography as a 'natural' bedfellow is because the islands, the pieces of land, remain central to his conception of the past experience of these places. I wish to argue in the remainder of this book that an interpretation of communities on islands which starts from the land is immediately biased towards an island model. What we really need, I propose, is *an archaeology of the sea* that incorporates the land rather than only merges with an 'archaeology of the land' as proposed by islandscapes. Such an archaeology of the sea would incorporate islands, or at least parts of the larger ones, and the seascape and the littoral of larger land masses, the continents. The focus would shift from the material and environment to an exploration of the lives of mariners and the communities from which they derive. The interest should be in the people who create the material and perceive the environment rather than the other way around.

CONCLUSION

In this chapter, I have provided a historical overview of the means by which the study of the archaeology of islands has been one which has focussed on the island as a piece of land which provides the unit of analysis. We have identified some of the problems inherent in this perception and identified the requirement to develop an archaeology of the sea in order to fully contextualise island existences in the past that are not restricted to islands. In Chapter 3, I wish to develop more fully an archaeology of the sea in order that the case studies can be considered as first attempts to develop maritime prehistories from the perspective of the sea, rather than pieces of land.

3

An Archaeology of the Sea

In this chapter, I wish to explore the ways in which the sea may be embodied and materialised through the practice of everyday life and as such how this may be used to our advantage in developing an archaeology of the sea. To achieve this, I ask the question what is special and different about being a member of a maritime community? This requires an understanding, derived from ethnographic, sociological and historical studies, of how a phenomenology or embedded perception of the sea may be embodied and, perhaps more importantly, identified in material culture. This takes the chapter beyond vision, so often a preoccupation with studies in landscape and other forms of archaeology (see Hamilakis 2001 and forthcoming and Rainbird 2002b and forthcoming for further discussion of this issue) and considers the context of differential synaesthesia derived through the practical historical experience of social actors. Issues of maritime-linked material culture are then considered. Having explored these, a preliminary consideration is given to how such embodiments of the seas might be identified as an archaeology of the sea.

The sea is a knowable place. In the same way that landscapes have to be understood also as visionscapes, soundscapes, touch-scapes and smellscapes (Tilley 1999), the sea is a textured place. A person approaching the sea from the land in a strong onshore breeze can attest to the bitter taste of salt that is driven by the wind into the mouth and drying the throat, providing both a 'tastescape' and a physical reaction. The textures of the sea are nuanced and utterly knowable places for those people who exist in them. In Micronesia, modern ethnography allied to historical reports provide an abundance of information that illustrates that through senses, lore, observation, technology, skill, mythology and myriad other ways the ocean of the Caroline Island seafarers was, and in some cases still is, a place that can be described, sung and mapped. The sea, in its form and texture, and its link with the guiding heavens are part of the everyday. It also connects the strange place that is always beyond the knowable world, the horizon, where the spirits of below meet the spirits of above in a cosmological understanding passed from one generation to the next (Goodenough 1986). This is a seascape traversed by known seaways, a place of paths that linked communities. I will return to this below, but first, I need to con-sider the issue of what, if anything, constitutes a maritime cultural landscape.

MARITIME CULTURAL LANDSCAPES

Since Christer Westerdahl's (1992, 1994) papers defining the mar-itime cultural landscape, some attention has been paid to trying to understand how the premises of terrestrial landscape archaeology may also be applied to the maritime realm. The majority of the world's surface is covered by sea and much of the land could be defined as located in littoral areas where land and sea meet. Such work to link maritime and terrestrial archaeologies has usefully been reviewed by A. J. Parker, in which he concludes that '[a]n appreciation of the maritime aspects of the historic landscape requires archaeologists to adopt a mariner's perspective...; (2001: 39). A 'mariner's perspective' would seem to be key to understanding the world as experienced by maritime communities, both on and off the land, but those considering maritime communities do not appear to accept that communities can be distinctly maritime, but rather that they must form only a component of society more generally.

John Hunter's (1994) critique of maritime cultural landscapes relies in part on analogy, and he mocks what would be an attempt to define an 'airborne culture' from a study of material culture elements such as airport locations, 'aircraft typology, hangars, runway configurations and duty free shops, not to mention aircraft disaster sites as being the direct equivalent of maritime wrecks' (1994: 262). Hunter goes on to argue that the different sensations and experiences of fliers and mariners do no more than enhance a 'broader cultural *persona*'. Parker (2001) agrees with the contention of Hunter (1994) that seafaring and seafarers are nothing more than components of a society more generally. Parker, taking an apparently functionalist view of society, states: 'What we are concerned with is **specialisation** within a society or community, and there is no guarantee that specialised **functions** will leave traces in the material culture record' (2001: 25, emphases in original).

It is not the place to go into detail here, but even at the time Hunter was writing the construct of culture was already being deconstructed and eschewed in anthropology and elsewhere, and such critiques often came from similar arguments that questioned the utility of notions of function and specialisation (epiphenomena) of coherent societies, that is, cultures. Our present concerns are more with perception and how experience alters the individual's understanding of the world. In archaeology we have become comfortable with the notion that material culture has an effect on how someone experiences the world and in so doing is always in a state of becoming a knowledgeable person. So Parker's conclusion quoted above that a 'mariner's perspective' is required is what I intend to explore here, by placing embodied experience at the forefront of interpretation, to show how people associated with sea can be distinct in comparison to a wider society through different perception of the world. This, in turn, creates self-reinforcing identities distinct from others not associated with maritime communities on a daily basis. Because perception of the landscape is learnt through experience, there may indeed be a distinct maritime landscape, or seascape, or perhaps better a community that draws its understandings of the world through associations with the sea as much or more than the land.

MARINERS AND MARITIME COMMUNITIES

Kirby and Hinkkanen (2000: 187) in their study of the Baltic and the North Seas find that seafarers, although not unique in being a distinct occupational group, have characteristics that make them different as:

> there is much in their way of life that reinforces the notion of them as a race apart. Separated for long periods of time from family and friends, and from the general pulse of human activity on land, they have perforce to create and live within their own shipboard society, with its own rules, codes and language . . . the sea is 'in their blood.'

Westerdahl (2005) has described how in northern Europe, seafarers used a different language while at sea which was distinct from that used on the land. Indeed, some land-based terms were regarded as *noa*, or taboo, and using them on board was regarded as bringing the potential for bad luck. The belief in taboo items also meant that things that could not be named at sea ought not to be taken on board either. These taboo items included women, children, agricultural implements and produce, stone, clergymen, domestic animals, cats, wolves, bears, foxes, hares, rabbits, otters, mice and rats. Clearly, in practice, such a wide range of taboo items could not be avoided, and indeed there are contradictions; for example, cats and dogs could bring luck to a boat and cats could catch mice and rats that had ventured aboard and dogs are known to have aided navigation in thick mist by reacting to the sound of dogs barking on shore (Westerdahl 2005). Dogs' acute sense of smell may also have been useful as the smells of the land are distinct from those of the sea. Rats and mice also are useful as an emergency food supply, especially as those who worked at sea were not supposed to eat the products of the sea while aboard. However, Westerdahl (2005) finds that much of the power of the taboo was in the conscious breaking of it.

Much power could be derived from such actions, but only if others understood what was being enacted. Thus, the special language and taboos and their breaking allowed '[t]hese ritual acts [to] socialise the initiated person into the values of the community' (Westerdahl 2005: 8). These distinct practices, acquired by working at sea, meant that those of the sea bonded with one another in ways distinct from those of the land. But we are not talking about sea peoples here; the community is one that is in actuality land-based. Others have commented on the bodily disposition of mariners that includes half-open hands (ready to grab a rope or rail), sunburnt and rugged skin, wide step and a rolling gait, all of which distinguish the seafarer from the landlubber (Montin 1994). But it is not just life at sea that makes seafarers distinct; it is also the communities within which they reside when in port.

In assessing the evolution of the fishing village on the coast of south Devon, England, Harold Fox (2001) notes how the dwellings and fish cellars were squeezed between the agricultural land of the manor and the high tide mark. In circumstances where rental documents exist, it is clear that the majority of the dwellings in these villages were landless. The communities in these circumstances had their backs to the land and their toes virtually in the sea. Of course, elsewhere, maritime exploits might be seasonal with seafarers periodically working the land. However, coast dwellers have often been conceived of as being in a marginal space and on the edge of 'civilisation'. Prior to the eighteenth century move towards seaside leisure resorts in Jutland, contemporary commentators suggested of the inhabitants that they 'differed from their inland neighbours in their build, their dialect, their clothing and their physiognomy' (Kirby and Hinkkanen 2000: 51).

Port towns are distinctive, they face the ocean, and are likely to be multi-cultural, but also divided. For example, in nineteenth-century Boulogne, France, residents of the maritime quarter used a special language, a '*patois des marins*' (Lee 1998). And Parker (1999) notes for Bristol, England, that there was a distinction made between the users of the muddy river and those that sailed on the open sea. Since the middle of the twentieth century, the requirements to service ships with deep draft and the extra space necessary for trans-shipment machines and the large containers in which much cargo is packed mean that the docks are no longer located in close proximity to residential areas, thus dispersing the tight-packed and close-knit maritime communities of historical times.

On the Pacific rim, colonial demands led rapidly to the development of what Ross Gibson (1994) has coined for early colonial Sydney 'ocean settlement', a mix of settler and diasporic communities, that is, numbers of people born of the fusion of diverse ancestry, with an entanglement of geographies and experiences realised through a European frame of governance. Anthony Pagden (1993) has noted that the long-distance seafarer took their home world with them aboard ship. The seafarer's existence was transferred from home port to ship, making each place a familiar space, but on reaching a distant land this familiarity was immediately challenged. However, as Gibson notes of ocean settlement, port towns in their diversity of humanity and the requirements of seafarers and shipping are familiar. It might be worth returning to popular literature at this point. Herman Melville, who spent time as a sailor, writes in *Moby Dick*, first published in 1851, of the character, or rather, the characters to be found in port towns:

> In thoroughfares nigh the docks, any considerable seaport will frequently offer to view the queerest looking nonde-scripts from foreign parts. Even in Broadway and Chest-nut Streets, Mediterranean mariners will sometimes jostle the affrighted ladies. Regent Street is not unknown to Las-cars and Malays; and at Bombay, in the Apollo Green, live Yankees have often scared the natives. . . .But in New Bed-ford, actual cannibals stand chatting at street corners; savages outright; many of whom yet carry on their bones unholy flesh. It makes a stranger stare. (1967: 37)

Ray (2003) has established the diversity of the seafaring communities plying the western Indian Ocean from prehistory to historic times. Classical and later authors describe Nabataeans, Sabaeans, Homerites, Arabs, Indians and Greeks. Using the evidence from an eyewitness source Ray also notes, in relation to pearl fishers on the coast of India in the sixteenth century, that the establishment of a community could be short-lived:

> The banks along the fisheries on the Indian coast were unin-habited, but the arrival of the fishing fleets in the 'period of transition between the two monsoons' completely trans-formed the place. 'A whole city of cottages made of wood and palm leaves stretched out for three hours along the beach'. In addition to divers, sailors, ship-owners, traders in pearl, var-ious entrepreneurs and merchants descended on the place. A wide variety of garb could be seen. (Ray 2003: 54)

What I hope to have established, albeit briefly, is that mariners and maritime communities are perceivably different to other types of community. In their difference, which may be a product of diversity, there can be a self-reinforcing identity that makes them perceptibly different from other individuals and communities.

BEING ON THE SEAS

For the navigators of the western Pacific, the sea was inculcated as part of the person, with the chanting and dancing involved in learning seaways making it a very physical presence. But more than this, in assessing currents or refracted waves caused by the presence of islands while at sea, the navigator may sense this through having their foot dipped in the water over the side of the boat or indeed, on occasion, it is reported that they would dangle their body over the side and sense the movement of the sea through their testicles (Lewis 1994). Of course, this was all combined in a synaesthetic, that is, a multiple sensory manner, to include apprehension of clouds, winds, birds and other phenomena. The boat itself was an extension of the human body, in that every roll and pitch was full of meaning to the practised mariner. Navigating by the prevailing currents was as typical for the Atlantic as it was the Pacific (Wooding 1996; Lewis 2004). In the Pacific Ocean experimental voyaging and revised scholarship have provided considerable support for the view that knowledgeable actors had considerable skills in traversing long distances between islands (e.g., Finney 1998; Gladwin 1970; Irwin 1992; Lewis 1994; see Chapter 5).

Taking to the sea is not without its dangers, and the large amount of recorded ritual relating to seafaring in the Micronesian sea of islands has as much to do with safe return as with successful, in an economic sense, trading or fishing expeditions. On the island of Kosrae in the eastern Caroline Islands, the hulls of the sailing vessels were painted red with the pigment derived from an inland location locally understood to be associated with menstruating women. Such women were regarded a danger to safe seafaring and were not allowed on the craft or near sailors who were soon to go to sea (see discussion in Rainbird 2004). It appears here that the situation as described by

Westerdahl above is occurring with a taboo item transformed into a powerful protective one by its conscious manipulation. Journeys were taken only when perceived safe to do so and the wind and weather were carefully contemplated before a decision to leave. Voyages were not a mere necessity for the collection and exchange of mundane goods, but were instead part and parcel of communities who did not always perceive their boundaries as being at the edge of their island. At other times, for example, when the Spanish settled Guam in the late seventeenth century, islanders broke off the connections that had existed along well-traversed seaways (see Rainbird 2004).

Evidence for the ability of people to read seas and weather is, of course, not restricted to Micronesia. Local conditions are best known to those who use those seas regularly, and practices would change accordingly. We find confirmation of such in the description of a *nakhoda* or mariner on a Red Sea *zarook* who 'never took bearings . . . he kept his eyes open, he knew his ship, and his life had been spent in the Red Sea [which] was to him as familiar as a well-lit street on a citizen's homeward journey' (Villiers 1954, quoted in Ray 2003: 19).

Whether pilotage may have been used in prehistory is a matter for conjecture, but pilots are typical of maritime communities in more recent times. The coast-hugging navigation proposed for much seafaring in the Mediterranean would not, for example, be a prudent method of navigating the western shores of Atlantic Europe, where the prevailing westerly conditions would serve to push the craft onto the shore. In the Atlantic, the winter was the least likely time for voyaging due to increased storminess, and is no doubt one of the reasons the monks of Lindisfarne on the coast of northeast England were surprised by a Viking attack in January 793 (Carver 1990).

Mariners working without 'satnav' and using only dead reckoning (an ability to identify their position) relied on a combination of factors. At night the stars and prevailing direction of swell or current could be used, and perhaps specific onshore lights may be

4. Le Pinacle, Jersey. This coastal feature acted as a focus for activity from the Neolithic period through to the end of the Iron Age. Its distinctive shape may have aided navigators (source author, 2004)

recognised. The Atlantic coasts have a profusion of small mediaeval chapels sited on what are often very exposed positions with a view of the sea where a light could be kept burning to aid mariners. Wooding (1996) notes a 'beacon hermitage' at Carn Brea in Cornwall, southwest England and opines that the early mediaeval burial sites at Tintagel in Cornwall and on Lundy in the Bristol Channel, in sight of Tintagel on a clear day, are both situated at locations suitable for a beacon to aid mariners and may indicate that such existed 1500 years ago. Of course, lighthouses are well known from classical times in the Mediterranean Sea and are a feature of Roman coastal architecture in the Atlantic sphere, as shown by the example at Dover in southeast England.

In daytime a number of other features of the maritime environment could be used in traversing the seaways; these are often called 'seamarks'. Of course, distinct coastal features, like high cliffs, specific peaks, notches in the cliffs, waterfalls, river mouths and other physical features, are typically used in identifying position of the coasts (Figure 4). High cliffs or mountains do, of course, improve the chances of locating land by being observable from a distance; such features also typically attract clouds, further indicating their location at a greater distance. Clouds covering shallow water such as that found at reefs and lagoons can indicate the position of such features by their colour at the base reflecting the different colour of the shallow water. The colour of geological features can also be an aid, as has been noted for the distinctive red cliffs at Ferriby on the Humber Estuary in England, where they may 'form keystones in building narrative maps that could be passed on verbally between seafarers, including those who had not visited the area previously' (Chapman and Chapman 2005: 48).

Sea shoals and reefs can feature as seamarks as can the constitution of the seabed. In the late nineteenth century, a fisherman described how he navigated in the North Sea by the depth of the water and the nature of the constituents of the sea bed when probed (Kirby and Hinkkanen 2000). In other words, different sea bed sediment types constituted a below-surface map of the sea. Wooding (1996) notes the tradition of using sounding-leads for similar purposes in the ancient Mediterranean, but points out that its value is limited to those who have a detailed knowledge of the topography of the sea bed. In the Marshall Islands, where schooling in navigation was aided by 'stick charts' made from palm fronds or pandanus splines indicating the patterns of the sea with individual shells marking the location of islands, the meeting points of deflected swells and currents were essential seamarks for navigating between the islands (Spennemann 2005).

We have already seen how dogs may be an aid to navigation, but other species also played a role. Of these the most commonly cited is birds. Seabirds usually have specific maximum distances they fly from land and will return to their roost every evening, providing a direction indicator to the seafarer. Migratory birds will tell of perhaps longer distance landfalls and may have acted as a guide for the discovery of new lands and migrations of peoples across seas. Ray (2003) notes that in the Indian Ocean birds were taken to sea and released to indicate the direction of land, but also finds that specific types of fish and sea snakes could be used to indicate location. The behaviour of birds and sea snakes also provided indications of impending weather conditions. In the Caroline Islands of Micronesia, animals were put to similar use. In addition, certain mythical figures, such as a pair of porpoises or a solitary white-tailed tropic bird, would also provide the *palu*, the initiated navigator, with an indication of position between islands (Gladwin 1970).

THE SEA(S) AND PHENOMENOLOGY

If the seas can be accepted as having similar attributes to landscapes, in that they have pathways and recognisable features, then it should be possible to develop a phenomenology of the sea(s) (cf. Tilley 1994). I am not advocating a universal phenomenology here; I am thinking rather more along the lines explained in *American Anthropologist* by Murphy Halliburton (2002). In this, through a study of Indian philosophies and ethnography he argues for local phenomenologies that are 'historically and culturally constructed . . . constituted by both local analytic theories of experience and lived experience itself and assume [that] these influence one another to some degree' (2002: 1126).

So, although the seascape is the linking factor between mariners, the way that seas are perceived at different times and places will be the result of local beliefs and practices. This, of course, ties in with Tim Ingold's (2000) critique of the anthropology of the senses, which highlights practical experience creating different perceptions of the world even within single societies.

The atoll-dwelling seafaring Caroline Islanders of Micronesia in the Pacific, following from the pioneering ethnographic work of Thomas Gladwin (1970), have been the focus of a number of attempts to understand what appears to be a different perceptive mapping of the world compared to that recorded elsewhere. For example, Alfred Gell (1985) found that the *etak* system of the Puluwat islanders described by Gladwin, which incorporates the oft-quoted notion that the navigator perceives himself and craft to be in a stable position with the island of departure moving away and the destination island moving towards them, is one of a token-indexical belief system. This type of system is typical of non-instrument way finding in all cases, but this does not diminish the fact that the world is being perceived quite differently even if the underlying logic to achieve the task can be regarded as the same.

Also drawing from Pacific ethnography and records of experimental voyaging in 'traditional' craft, Don Ihde (1993: 100) has described such way finding across the seascape as an 'embodied position system' where the sea is said to 'pass by us' rather than the boat going through the sea. Here Ihde is highlighting the nature of bodily position and perception where the body (and it has often been said that the navigator's body extends through the boat as all its movements are sensed) becomes the fixed point, while the environment works around it rather than following a pathway through the environment.

Ihde's use of the term 'embodiment' brings me to the crux of the matter because the distinction that has been drawn between seafaring people and others is one that, although often expressed as a visual perception of difference in regard to demeanour, clothes and so on, is one that must be embodied in a variety of senses. That is, a certain combination of sensory registers, creating a synaesthesia, must be derived from practical experience in a particular place and time (Sutton 2001).

Before pursuing the issue of synaesthesia further, I need first to consider what is meant by embodiment. Although Halliburton (2002) notes that the term embodiment is used by many to merely indicate a focus on the body, it is the definition provided by Thomas Csordas (1999) that more closely matches my usage here. He says the body 'is a biological, material entity and embodiment is an indeterminate methodological field defined by perceptual experience and by mode of presence and engagement in the world' (1999: 182). Although I am not sure that I understand the use of 'methodological' in the context of this quote, it certainly has to be the case that the experience through presence and engagement in the world is the necessary focus for any understanding of mariners and members of maritime communities.

MATERIAL CULTURE, GENDER AND PRACTICAL EXPERIENCE

David Howes (2003) identifies the need to explore the interplay of the senses, rather than each individually, and it is this complete bodily understanding of being to which Chris Gosden refers in introducing a volume dedicated to the study of archaeology and aesthetics. Here Gosden (2001: 163) finds that:

> Material culture affects us through our senses, especially if we include our haptic sense which allows our bodies to work on and in the world in a muscular, physical manner. Our sensory apprehension of the world is not purely a physiological matter of impulses reaching the brain from the body, but rather it is something we have to engage in actively, albeit unconsciously. Making sense, as the verb implies, is an active process. The locus of sensory activity is as much cultural as bodily, so that various cultures apprehend the world in different ways.

Archaeologists of the sea need to identify maritime-related material culture, which can include such things as harbours/quays, docks, cranes, warehouses/cellars, boat sheds/houses, defences (sea and military), fishing gear and communal works (as it generally takes more than one person to operate a boat, etc.). There is an inscription of meaning created through such buildings and the activities that occurred there, which are inscribed in all the senses and linked through bodily adornment by the addition of broad knives, special clothes and tattoos. Prehistorians are unlikely to find a suite of such items, but that distinctive elements of material culture figured in the existence of communities cannot be doubted. The boat, for example, is a very rare find, but we have to start with the assumption that it existed and most likely in a form not found in landlocked communities. Once the boat is acknowledged, then a whole suite of related items of material culture must be assumed for the maintenance and operation of such craft. This material culture and its practical and symbolic uses will constitute a distinctive community. Identifying marks may include flags, and perhaps distinctive colours or symbols on sails where they are used, but also less physical forms of material culture such as songs and shanties, the specifics of vocabulary, as discussed above, and gender distinctions.

In the Caroline Islands of Micronesia matrilineality, the tracing of clan ancestry through the female line from mother to child, and land ownership through the clan, is often flagged as a singular feature of these societies within Oceania. Margaret Jolly (2001) has made the point that in the Caroline atolls, with land passing through the mothers, women are linked to the land and men to the sea. The female roots to the land should not be expressed as indigeneity as opposed to routes, in a James Clifford (1997) sense, as a synonym for diaspora. In the Caroline Islands it might be best to conceive of roots and routes as both local and indigenous, in a place where this is a gender distinction rather than an economic or geographic one. If the endorsement of land (not forgetting that tenure extends across reef and sea as well) exists with women, then the realm of the sea, in the male role as navigators and travellers, is another local means to power. Such relationships are worked out in different ways politically at the local scale (see Petersen 1999), but as Jolly (2001: 431) states in relation to both past and present forms of travel, 'motivated mobility is good, especially for men. Past exchanges between islands in canoes, even shipboard journeys as indentured labourers and contemporary migrations to town . . . are seen as potentially empowering journeys, for men at least.'

Other assumed gender roles in maritime communities can be distinct from those in contemporary neighbouring landlocked communities. It could be argued that the role of women in such communities is a very powerful one in having to take on the role of head of the household during the absence of their male partners at sea. Men, if they had long periods in all-male crews, learned domestic skills that when applied at home would have more normally been regarded as female activities (Kirby and Hinkkanen 2000). Indeed, standard gender conventions are often transformed by those linked to the sea in popular Western thought, but female power may be enhanced in being the constant household representative on land (Lee 1998). As Westerdahl (2005) illustrates, there may be specific gendering of roles; however, the actual biological sex of the participant does not necessarily have to coincide with the ideal practice; that is, the sexes may be interchangeable.

Departures and homecomings often linked to seasonality may be major events leading to an emotional ritualised seascape. This seascape of departures and hoped for arrivals is one of intimate relations between person, seascape and sea craft. The seascape is familiar terrain and the knowledgeable and initiated, as pointed out above, can read the seamarks, the most obvious of which are outcropping reefs and rocks, but others may be subsurface or even mythological. Within this spatial domain, as indicated by comings and goings, is a temporal one, or at least this is often assumed. Much discussion of time in relation to the sea, other than considerations in relation to seasonality, concerns the likely duration of journeys by sea craft. Although this can usefully show that journeys by sea may be preferred to land as reducing significantly the time required to complete it (e.g., Carver 1990), the duration of a journey may not actually be a significant consideration. Christos Doumas (2004: 220) writing of sea journeys by islanders in the Aegean says, '[t]arget is paramount in the hierarchy of values, while time is of little consequence'. I have often heard people talk of 'island time', a sense that things will be done in the end, the target will be achieved so there is no need to worry about it right now. This lack of urgency is perhaps part of an attraction for people holidaying on islands and a source of frustration to outsiders from societies where 'time means money'. The relativity of time is a well-researched and recognised subject and 'island time' is not restricted to islands. One can imagine that the goals of the type of journey remarked upon by Doumas will also have the desirability of regular ports of call, the rekindling or reinforcing of alliances and kinship ties. Hospitality in maritime communities would be a reciprocal affair played out over generations rather than billing periods. Such a situation may work well in the Mediterranean, but there is a temporal prerogative at work in other maritime communities that relates to the tide.

In the communities of the Atlantic, for example, the tide which changes twice a day and goes through further annual cycles of extremes will have a significant effect on when journeys could take place and what routes were available. Time in these communities may be more important and include considerations not only of time of departure, but also time of arrival if a particular tide was necessary for the approach to the destination. In relation to that discussed above, the local phenomenological context will be different where tides are significant features of the sea.

■ INTIMATE RELATIONS

The naming of sea craft can create links to shore and kin and these linkages, whether conscious or not, can be taken to any point on the seas. Dwyer, Just and Minnegal (2003: 19) find in their study of contemporary fishing communities in southeast Australia:

> [e]ach boat, in its own right, is secured through its name to the relationships embodied in that name; an umbilical connection to home and hearth. All of those boats, collectively, through the individuals who have been and are linked through the names, socialise the sea; they give it dimensions it would not otherwise have, and establish the sense of both time and place.

Intimate relations with sea craft through manufacture and naming also are further inscribed through the rituals particular to seafaring; these range from prohibitions on sexual intercourse prior to voyaging proscribed in parts of Micronesia to the broad Western avoidance of whistling on modern motor vessels in order to avoid calling up a wind (of course, the opposite occurred on sailing vessels that had been caught in a calm). Sea craft and the intimate and specialised knowledge of construction create a bond between sailors and craft (Kirby and Hinkkanen 2000: 99, 100). Across Oceania this is exemplified by the use of body metaphors for naming elements of the vessel structure. The traditional sea craft of Oceania, often called canoes in common parlance, are sophisticated machines developed through the accretion of the actions of knowledgeable actors over millennia in maritime communities, a scenario that Greg Dening (2003: 204–205) enthusiastically endorses:

> Sixteen hundred generations had produced an artefact of extraordinary genius. A canoe. Believe me. That vehicle, which could sail across thousands of miles of the Great Ocean, was a thing of cultural genius. Genius in the sail that dispensed with the need of a rudder and could take it into the wind. Genius in the caulking and internal lugging that made its planked sides flexible and waterproof. Genius in its outrigger and the asymmetric moulding of its sides. Genius in the platform across the double canoe that could carry forty to one hundred people, the fire pit, shelter and tons of cargo. Genius in its making and ownership. Genius in its navigation. No wonder the canoe became an icon and metaphor of greatness through the Sea of Islands.

The practical experience of engaging with the sea, building and setting off on sea craft and dwelling in maritime communities must lead to differences between communities that do engage and those that do not, and these differences should be the subject of archaeology.

ARCHAEOLOGIES OF THE SEA(S)

Archaeologically the hardest people to identify through material remains will be sea-nomads, now almost exclusively found in the islands of Southeast Asia. People living wholly on the sea may have been more widespread in times past. Certainly the Phoenicians who inhabited the fringes of the Mediterranean Sea some 3500 to 2500 years ago have been likened to sea-nomads and their history difficult to discern archaeologically. French philosophers Gilles Deleuze and Félix Guattari (1988) developed a 'treatise on nomadology' in considering how nomads are concerned more with the space in-between rather than the specific points that are the concern of sedentary people; they live in 'smooth space' unhindered by the 'striated' space of walls, enclosures and roads of sedentary peoples. The lack of friction means they are not required to move. Territory is their place; they are not migrants moving to another place. 'It is not surprising that reference has been made to spiritual voyages effected without a relative movement, but in intensity, in one place: these are part of nomadism' (Deleuze and Guattari 1988: 381). A feature of smooth space, that is, nomad space, is the 'polyvocality of directions' that are available. For the Mediterranean, Horden and Purcell (2000) have noted the advantage of islands in having a connectivity in all directions; it is the sea not the island which allows this. Deleuze and Guattari continue by finding that the sea is smooth space and as such is a territory which expands horizons rather than reduces them. We should be aware of the metaphorical use of some of these terms; the sea is not always smooth, but it is a space for movement. This recalls the islanders of Puluwat Atoll with their perception when sailing that they did not move, but that islands moved towards and past them. Thus, following Deleuze and Guattari, the Pulawatese are conceptually not required to move because the sea is their territory.

Those who live with the seas may be regarded as having a keen perception of the elements, a willingness, at some level, to participate in the community organisation of labour and, most importantly, an expectation of continual encounter with otherness, at home or elsewhere (Figure 5). These histories of the sea are embodied in the individual and the community, and this embodiment is related to both perception and experience of the environment and the specifics of material culture linked to the sea. It must be an essential aim of

5. People of the sea meet those of the land. Volos, Greece (source author, 2005)

those dealing with such societies to identify how the sea is embodied in the specific temporal and spatial context of study. Exploring maritime communities rather than island or coastal societies conceptually decentres the land and replaces the sea as the arena for deriving an understanding of people from littoral areas, whether they be situated on island, continent or somewhere in between. What I contend is that we require a shift from the metaphors of island equals isolated and sea equals barrier, and in so doing we will open up a world of interpretative opportunities.

FACING THE SEA

It is apparent that before the evolution of our own species, hominids had found a way to successfully colonise land across water as we now know that *Homo erectus* managed to inhabit the island of Flores in the Indonesian Archipelago (Morwood et al. 1999). Certainly, post-Pleistocene, and in a few places earlier (e.g., Island Melanesia as will be discussed in Chapter 5), 'locomotion' (as Evans termed it) was likely quite sophisticated. The presence of sea-going vessels meant that humans were not always limited to their pieces of land, except perhaps when forced upon them by the vagaries of season, tide, wind or weather. In many places the island region would be extended and would incorporate a sea that was as familiar, or more familiar, than the land they left. In such circumstances social choice must be responsible for the maintenance of external contacts or attempts to deny them.

The environment and geography have a big part to play in all of this and will have both facilitating and constraining effects on sea travel. For example, Ferdinand Braudel (1972) made it clear to us that the Mediterranean Sea is a complex of seas and should not be treated as a unity. These seas within a sea each have distinctive histories, and the islands and coastlines which are connected by their waters will have played varying roles. As Braudel (1972: 150) states, 'it was impossible to sail far in the Mediterranean without touching land.' This will be discussed further in the next chapter, but I prefer to see the Mediterranean seas as, in Geoff Irwin's (1992) term, potential 'nurseries' for the development of maritime technology and navigation. Irwin has identified the sea defined by the Bismarck Archipelago, the Bismarck Sea, as the 'voyaging nursery' that led 3500 years ago to the settlement of the Pacific islands. The 'nursery' conditions are identified by a favourable configuration of islands and other land masses which allow for the relatively safe experimentation with sailing and navigating, allowing for technological innovation and the knowledge and experience to travel beyond the nursery when the time is right. In the next few chapters I will consider the issue of voyaging or sailing nurseries in relation to other locations.

People inhabiting shores have been seafaring successfully for millennia, even prior to the evolution of our own species. Islands, in Western tradition, have become regarded as places where strange and exotic people and things reside. The common use of the island metaphor for isolated communities, wherever they may be located, has led to a general acceptance by archaeologists of models that emphasize the bounded landscape at the expense of broader horizons. We need to accept that people were at home with the sea, as pointed out in the Dening quote above; they could take their hearth with them. In the next four chapters I aim to develop archaeologies of the seas for the prehistories of the four island regions introduced in Chapter 1.

4

The Mediterranean

Malta

A s I have shown in the previous chapters, the islands of the Mediterranean Sea have made a significant contribution in being used to develop a notion of a distinctive island archaeology. It is appropriate then that the first case study chapter should focus on this sea and in particular the islands of Malta which are central to both the sea and many of the ideas developed about island communities as isolated and distinctive in prehistory.

■ MALTA

The Maltese islands are located in the central Mediterranean Sea some 80 kilometres south of Sicily and less than 300 kilometres from the African coast. The islands are

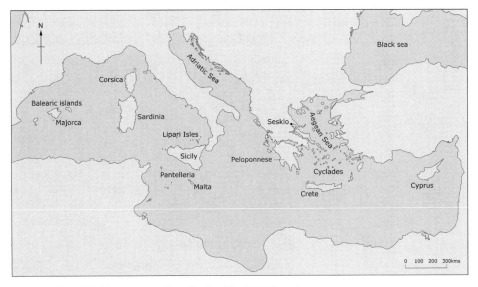

6. Map of the Mediterranean Sea (drafted by H. Wilson)

situated on what is, for the most part, a submerged ridge running from North Africa to Sicily, which provides the division between the western and eastern basins of the Mediterranean Sea (Figure 6). The islands themselves consist of two large islands separated by an 8-kilometres wide stretch of water (Figure 7). Malta is the larger of the two with maximum dimensions of 28 kilometres long and 13.5 kilometres wide and an area of about 237 square kilometres. Gozo is 14.5 kilometres long and 7 kilometres wide with an area of 66 square kilometres. These, along with a number of much smaller islands which make up the group, are formed by two types of limestone; the earliest is Coralline which is overlain by Globigerina, and topped in most parts of the islands by clay and marl.

The evidence from excavations of the lowest levels at Skorba indicates that the islands appear to have been settled by humans in the Neolithic at approximately 5000 BC (Trump 2002). These settlers brought with them cattle, sheep/goats, barley, emmer and naked wheat and lentils. Earlier visits may have been responsible for the demise of the endemic fauna which included pygmy elephant and hippopotamus, but the settlers of the Neolithic may have accounted for the extinction of the endemic red deer. There appears to be no

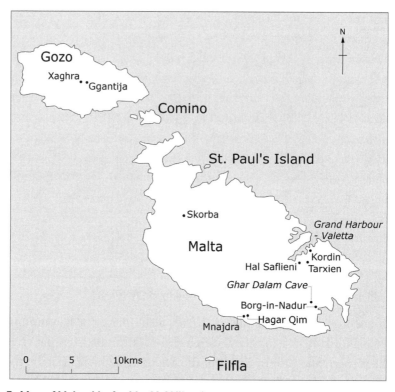

7. Map of Malta (drafted by H. Wilson)

dispute, as established by pottery types and stone imports, that the settlers derived from communities in Sicily and maintained contacts with them throughout the early phase (5000–3500 BC).

Given there are thousands of islands in the Mediterranean, and indeed many much larger ones than Malta, it is the distinctive Neolithic remains that have attracted archaeologists to make bold claims about distinctive island propensities derived from isolation and insularity. These distinctive remains come in the form of megalithic monumental architectural remains of free-standing buildings built to a common plan and two associated underground complexes at Hal-Saflieni on Malta proper and the other at Xaghra on Gozo. The above-ground examples, of which at least fourteen complexes are known (and many more suspected), are usually termed temples based on convincing analyses of their ground plans, architectural features, stone furniture, statuary and assemblages of artefacts. The temples and the underground chambers share few parallels with anything known elsewhere at this time. The common plan of the temples is to have a concave façade with central entrance door leading directly to the central line of axis with lobe-shaped rooms placed symmetrically on either side (left and right). The thickness of the external wall conceals the internal plan and often incorporates other spaces entered by small doors carved in the limestone. A lobe may also form the end of the central axis, the furthest extent of the temple, sometimes referred to as the 'holy of holies'. The simplest temple form consists of three lobes creating a trefoil plan in character. Temples could have between three and six lobes. In some cases, later modifications have introduced a secondary axis corridor and demolished parts of earlier structures, a good example being the main temple at Hagar Qim (Figure 3).

The temple sites have been dated as constructed through the period from c. 3600 to 2500 BC. Their attribution as Neolithic is thus very late in regard to the chronology of the lands to the north and east where copper metalworking technology was in use by this time. There is no evidence of metal work related to the temples of Malta, and this is shared in Europe at this time by the inhabitants of Britain, Ireland and Scandinavia. For Malta, it is this perceived backwardness which has led archaeologists to propose that the temples must have been a unique development of islanders in isolation, a cultural elaboration leading to exaggerated development as Evans would have termed it. The proposition is put simply that the expectation would not be to find these elaborate monuments on small islands unless the physical isolation determined by the sea creates an inward-looking, competitive and extremely religious society. Simon Stoddart and colleagues (1993) thought they could identify cycles of isolation and openness, with temple building being a response to isolation. Interestingly, as part of this model they also observed that the orientation of the temples, if defined as the direction from the main entrance to the innermost part of the temple, was with few exceptions north and northwest, the directions of Sicily and the obsidian sources at Lipari and Pantelleria. Lipari is in the Aeolian Islands off the north coast of Sicily and Pantelleria is located 110 kilometres southwest of Sicily in the direction of the African coast at Tunisia, to which it is geographically closer. This reversal of a trend which normally asks us to consider the orientation of architecture by looking out through the entrance (still common for Malta; cf. Tilley 2004) may indicate a concern by the temple builders that they marked the islands of origin for their ancestors and the direction from which exotic stone was imported. The periods of openness in Maltese prehistory were identified through the presence of obsidian and isolation by its absence, but the authors stressed that these were preliminary findings. These sources of obsidian were being exploited from the beginning of the Neolithic and have been found not only in Malta, but also in southern Europe and North Africa, standing as proxy testament to the ability of seafarers at this time (Trump 2002). The temples then rather appear to ossify a link with travel over the sea, rather than provide an indication of insularity.

So the notion of the supposed isolation of the Maltese group during the temple phase is not without its contradictions. Another similarity and difference is the distinctive nature of the architecture in itself. Megalithic monumental architecture is not unknown in other Mediterranean islands and the lands to the north of the sea, but the temples are unique. They are innovative in being free standing, not requiring earth and rocks as buttresses (apart from where what appear to be repairs are apparent), and apart from the underground examples they appear to be constructed for use by living people, rather than sepulchres for the dead, which is usual for megalithic architecture elsewhere in the region. The question and point is why create a distinctive architecture, one with a design which is followed with few modifications over a period of a thousand years, if it was only to be observed and experienced by the people who are familiar with it? Surely such consistency in difference is aimed at creating a cohesive identity with which to impress outsiders, those that are unfamiliar with the type and thus, through retellings of stories of the voyage can tell others of the distinctive achievements of the inhabitants of the 'islands of honey, floating in the sea' (Tilley 2004: 142).

John Robb (2001) has estimated that the sea gap between Sicily and Malta could be crossed in small boats, either rowed or sailed in calm summer conditions, in one to three days. Indeed, he suggests that it would have taken at least as long for communities on Sicily itself to visit each other if they chose to walk, a proposition Robb says would be the least preferred option. Should we not then see uniqueness and difference as more likely the result of creating and maintaining identity in the face of normal and continuing contacts with outsiders? This would also account for the continued import and use of obsidian and the rejection of metal. Further to this, could the monuments themselves act as attractors to the islands, which may otherwise be bypassed?

Sir Themistocles Zammit, the excavator of the Hypogeum of Hal-Saflieni and the temples of Tarxien, wrote during the period between the world wars:

> The numerous megalithic sanctuaries of the Maltese group indicate a sturdy primitive stock of people, peaceful and religious, who turned their hands to the erection of buildings to honour the unknown powers that held them in subjugation. In these temples, the navigator who approached the sheltered harbours offered sacrifices to propitiate the powers of the sea during a dangerous crossing. Malta was the holy island of neolithic faith, the half-way house of the early mariners, who trusted themselves to their frail wooden craft, full of hope in a protecting power.
>
> The mariners, guided by the natives, hied to the nearest sanctuary, where a fat bull or a humble goat was bled before the altar and burnt before the holy image. The oracle predicted a prosperous journey or the fulfilment of hopes and desires.
>
> Journeys to distant oracular caverns were common all along the Mediterranean lands in far later periods. The Hypogeum

of Hal-Saflieni and the temples of Tarxien precede all known oracular sites. Yet they were well adapted to inspire the visitor with awe, and with a deep sense of mystery and of the power of unseen spirits. The Hal-Saflieni caverns and the Tarxien temples may have attracted people from distant lands because of their belief in the power of the oracles which might be consulted in them. (Zammit 1930: 122–123)

Zammit's excavations had begun decades earlier when little was known about the spectacular remains of Malta and few had suspected the longevity or indeed, integrity, of survival (most often Phoenicians were regarded as responsible – the detail of early explorations may be found in Evans 1971). The picture Zammit paints of the Neolithic remains is one that, in part, conforms with post–World War II interpretations as further sites have been identified and excavated, but it also in many significant ways differs from the norm of depictions in the second half of the twentieth century in that Neolithic seafaring, although identified as potentially hazardous, is clearly regarded as normal practice. In becoming a holy island, as Zammit suggests here, the inhabitants of Malta not only may have benefited from the visits of mariners already plying trade through this part of the Mediterranean, but fame may also have led to pilgrimage.

Grima (2001) hints that temple complexes are placed between coastal embarkation points and the centre of the islands, while Stoddart (2002) has discussed the various features of the temple complexes on the Xaghra Plateau of Gozo and above the Grand Harbour at Tarxien. He proposed that there would have been processional routes to the complexes and between the various features of the temple complex landscape, and elsewhere the propitious nature of routes and pathways and the locales of development along their routes or for which the route was chosen has been the subject of much discussion (e.g., Tilley 1994), but little has been written about pilgrimage in prehistory. Pilgrimage in the modern world is normally associated with heavily theorised and dogmatised religion, but we should not imagine this for the ancient world. Pilgrims to the temples of Malta likely gained from their visits a huge variety of individual experience based on varied practice, beliefs, rituals and superstitions, the majority of which must have been gained through non-verbal communication. Even in the modern world, and where the expectations of most are derived from textual sources, anthropological studies have shown the profound differences in how holy places are conceptualised by pilgrims, with the ritual space providing a variety of opportunities for the expression of diversity of the perceptions and meanings imposed on the shrine by the pilgrims themselves (Eade and Sallnow 1991). The temples were certainly roofed, as plaster has been found on the walls and this is covered by imported red ochre (Trump 2002). The deep red wall, sculpted decoration and statuary would have been illuminated by the flickering flames of fires in hearths, the wood smoke perhaps augmented with a heady mix of scented herbs. Stoddart (2002) has discussed the potential role played by sound in these enclosed spaces and opined as to whether the stone bowls found in temple period sites may have been drums. In this environment of shadows and niches where glimpses revealed a further variety of spaces that may have been traversed or restricted to access in the most complex temples, it is not hard to imagine that the travellers and pilgrims would bring their own interpretations to the proceedings.

Accounts of pilgrimage usually confirm that locals rarely visit their local pilgrimage sites. So what then did attracting pilgrims to the islands offer the inhabitants of Malta beyond notoriety and an expanded potential gene pool? Offerings, however, are a normal part of pilgrimage activity, but given there is little regarded as exotic in nature to be found in artefact assemblages of this period in Malta, what might the pilgrims be presenting? Accounts of pilgrimage in the Classical World often refer to the offerings of a variety of food stuffs, for example, domesticated animals to be sacrificed or seed grains to be placed on the shrine (Coleman and Elsner 1995). Domesticated animals and seed would have been a useful supplement to the Maltese economy and an obvious tangible benefit to becoming a holy island.

Carvings of sheep, fish and cattle are known from temple sites along with pigs, including a sow with fourteen suckling piglets at Tarxien, perhaps representing some of the offerings made at these sites. Interior decoration at Tarxien also includes what has been interpreted as representations of sea craft; although less expertly carved than other interior decoration at this site, they show boat shapes in outline with some indications of oars or passengers and at least two appearing to depict masts. The most substantial depiction illustrates a solid-looking craft with steep bow with bowsprit and a flat stern; it also appears to show a large unfurled square sail in the midships (Trump 2002: 214; cf. Woolner 1957). The indication of sailing technology at this time is interesting and unique, but we appear here to have a direct representation of the transport necessary to pilgrims. To add to the carvings we also have the bones of the animals themselves where conditions have allowed. At Tarxien South what has been described as an altar located in the first apse right of the entrance had a niche behind, and this was full of animal bones. Below this niche, in a concealed cubby hole located within a panel of abstract carvings, was found a flint knife and goat horn core assumed to be related animal sacrifice (Trump 2002) (Figure 8).

Ray (2003) notes that the Indian Ocean in pre-modern times was the location of regular and routine passenger traffic of pilgrims. These pilgrims were on *hajj* to Mecca on voyages that 'cut across political boundaries' (2003: 15). He also notes the spread by sea of Buddhism from its founding home in the Indian sub-continent to the islands of Sri Lanka and those in Southeast Asia. Return trips for pilgrims for lay devotees and monks to visit locations associated with the life of Buddha were another requirement for sea travel.

An example of pilgrimage to islands, although this time in a 'vertical archipelago' of mountains, can provide a couple of useful insights to the posited situation of Malta. Brian Bauer and Charles Standish (2001) have made a detailed study of two islands in Lake Titicaca, a body of freshwater located in the Andes 3180 metres above sea level. The lake is very large, covering an area 8500 km^2,

8. 'Altar', Tarxien, Malta (source author, 2000)

and has attracted human settlement to its shores for millennia. Two islands located close to the Copacabana Peninsula at the southern edge of the lake are well recorded from early visitors and ethnographic evidence as the Island of the Sun and the Island of the Moon, creating a complex with shrines which probably made it the third most sacred place in the Inca world. The focus on these islands, as opposed to the many other islands in the lake (although these too probably had a lesser sacred status), is that the larger of the two islands, Titicaca, which has an area 20 km^2, was subject to the pan-Andean belief that here the sun and moon were born. People from all over the Inca Empire are recorded to have made pilgrimages to the 'Sacred Rock', a reddish sandstone outcrop located at a point on the islands furthest from the nearest shore, and reportedly embellished with cloth and precious metals. Here also a precinct was built and buildings which enhance an association with the setting sun of the summer solstice. Elsewhere on the island were elaborate shrines for pilgrims and settlements for the keepers of the sacred place, who also tended to the fields where maize was grown.

Bauer and Standish do not dwell on the requirement for pilgrims to cross the 1-kilometre water gap from the lake shore to the island except to note that the reed boat used for the crossing mediated the divide from an already sacred area on the peninsula to the most sacred place, being the island itself. The pilgrim route is clearly defined and many thresholds required crossing, the water just being one of them. Although we are talking here of a state-sponsored religion and this is not likely to compare to Neolithic Malta, the embellishment of the islands with architectural features does hold similarities with the temple-building of Malta. The second item which may have a bearing on our understanding of prehistoric Malta is that the maize grown on the Island of the Sun was in itself regarded as sacred and highly sought after by the pilgrims as bringing propitious luck to their own farming endeavours. At this altitude, maize was close to the limit of its cultivation range, but maize was not uncommon in the Inca Empire more generally, and was a staple crop. What we should recognise from this is that potentially mundane items can be transformed by association with a sacred place and such items will be hard to detect archaeologically. Perhaps a similar item, honey, for example, was a sought after product from Malta due to its sacred associations?

◼ SEAS WITHIN SEAS

Although Malta has taken on somewhat of an exaggerated status in
the development of a distinctive island archaeology for the purposes
of this study, it is best to go beyond the specifics of the particular
case study in order to establish the proxy evidence required to show
that the Mediterranean Sea was alive with mariners and maritime
communities in the Neolithic and Chalcolithic. To do this we need
to take a step back to look at the geography of the Mediterranean
for potential nurseries for seafaring and consider the palaeoenvironmental and archaeological evidence in relation to marine activities.

The Mediterranean Sea has a number of seas within it. We have
already noted that there are two large basins, the West and the East,
defined by a constriction at the centre where the islands of Malta are
located. In the eastern basin are the Adriatic and Aegean Seas. These
seas saw a great deal of change at the end of the Pleistocene; as sea
levels rose the Adriatic almost doubled in size as low-lying plain lands
at its northern end became submerged. The changes for the Aegean
due to sea level rise were rather different in that the expansion of the
sea was through low-lying valleys, thus creating the coastline we are
familiar with today. In both cases people would have lost land and
may have been constricted to new coastlines. In the Aegean, some
communities would have to cope with becoming islanders. Long-
held social associations may become divided by stretches of water
where hitherto land had existed.

Many communities would have become associated with the sea
in ways that had not previously been required, but we also know
that some people in this region had already built strong attachments to the sea. Here we turn to the evidence from Franchthi Cave.
Franchthi Cave in the Argolid region of the northeast Peloponnese
is located on what has always been part of the Greek mainland.
The finds from excavations here have revealed proxy data for early
seafaring on the edge of the Aegean 10,000 years ago as the obsidian found in the cave shows that people were making journeys to
collect it from the island of Melos (Jacobsen 1976; Cherry 1981).

The initial discovery of the obsidian source, and earliest visits to quarry it, would have been facilitated by the lower sea levels at the end of the Pleistocene. At this time the large island mass of 'Cycladia' would have enabled navigation along the coast between Franchthi and Melos with only a couple of open sea gaps of no more than a few kilometres (van Andel and Runnels 1987). In the Early Holocene sea level rose rapidly, and by 8000 years ago the large amount of Melos obsidian found at Franchthi indicates more substantial sea-crossings. This raw material exploitation may have been linked to the deep-sea fishing of tuna in distant, cold, nutrient-rich waters, as indicated by the faunal assemblage at Franchthi (van Andel and Runnels 1987). But at Franchthi and Lipari where Mesolithic exploitation of the obsidian source is also attested, the exploitation of obsidian appears to predate significant evidence of tuna fishing (Castagnino Berlinghieri 2002).

In reviewing the beginnings of the Neolithic in the Mediterranean, Alberto Cazzella (2002: 414) acknowledges that the introduction of domesticated plants and animals to new parts probably occurred by sea.

> Ever since the Early Neolithic when navigation skills were developed, or better still when [it was] decided to exploit this potential to the full, the Mediterranean with its particular configuration and the presence of peninsulas and islands, provided the ideal background for culture contacts . . .

The facilitation of the arrival of domesticated plants and sheep/goats in southeastern Europe at about 7000 BC, whether or not this was associated with the migration of people also, required some form of waterborne transport, if only to cross the Dardanelles, thus bridging the gap between Asia and Europe. Although the Mesolithic population of Greece may have been widely dispersed, the coast dwellers of the Aegean would have been well placed to do this given the seafaring technology and skill evident from Franchthi. From the Early Neolithic in northern Greece, we find obsidian from

Melos, and sites of this date in Southeast Europe typically contain beads and bracelets manufactured from *Spondylus* shell and sourced from the Aegean Sea. Alistair Whittle (1996) has commented how these are proxy indicators of the maintenance of long-range contacts between the early farming communities.

The Aegean Sea possesses the attributes to develop as a sailing nursery, a place where seafaring skills could be honed in relative security, as discussed in Chapter 3. The Aegean Sea is bounded by land on three sides, there are clusters of islands providing multiple landfalls and utility of sea craft, and accidental travel too far south would see the protective barrier of Crete. Unlike oceanic pioneers, Aegean navigators would also not have had to cope with a significant tidal range. As such, other than occasional tectonic events, the interface between sea and land was stable, providing secure knowledge of safe havens at any time of the day or night. Cyprian Broodbank (1999b, 2000) has researched the role of sailing nurseries in the colonisation of the Aegean Islands in detail.

Broodbank accepts that there was already a well-developed Mesolithic pattern of seafaring, but also acknowledges that for the most part evidence of settlement of the Aegean Islands does not occur until the Neolithic and usually towards the end of that period. Following Irwin, Broodbank considers the notion of sailing nurseries as areas for developing the skills which would allow for island settlement in the region. Although he recognises that the Aegean as a whole might be considered one such nursery, he prefers to identify two zones, where the combination of coast with sheltered bays and off-shore islands may promote a nursery environment. One stretches from Pagasitic Gulf in the north, through the strait separating the mainland and Euboia, around the Attica peninsula and incorporating the Argolid. The second encompasses a large stretch of the west Anatolian coast from Lesbos in the north to Rhodes in the south. These are interesting suggestions, and it makes sense that the earliest sea passages are made between the mainland and islands closest to the shore, but there is an issue of scale and chronology here. Of the nurseries proposed, it is clear from the distribution of

Melos obsidian that this area can already be regarded as in operation as a theatre for seafaring activities in the Mesolithic and Earliest Neolithic, but this is not well-attested by evidence from the islands in the region. It is also the case that if the earliest Neolithic settlement of Thessaly was by migrant farmers using sea craft, then immediately at the beginning of the Neolithic we are looking at voyages of much greater distance than those attested by the archaeology of the islands. As such, the entire Aegean Sea as a nursery, where these skills are developed over the long term, is, I think, rather more likely than the smaller areas Broodbank proposed.

Castagnino Berlinghieri (2003) has studied in detail the likely prevailing maritime conditions facing Mediterranean seafarers in the ancient past. In assessing wind, waves and currents, the three major influences on navigation she finds have changed little from the early Holocene period, and thus contemporary conditions can be used to assess the conditions of voyaging in the past. In regard to the Aeolian Islands, the analysis reveals that short-distance sailing to Sicily or mainland Italy could occur at any time of the year, but in concurring with classical authors finds that long-distance voyaging would be limited to the period of April to October, encompassing the months of high summer. The author also recognises that long-distance voyages would be rather more a series of shorter voyages requiring several ports of call along the way. Such a scenario obviously requires us to imagine that safe havens, both from storms and unfriendly people, were available and expected.

In regards to the Neolithic, how might we imagine these safe havens? We are not expecting docks and breakwaters, but rather must be looking for sheltered bays with shallow and wide shorelines where the boats could be beached. Certainly when considering the earliest Neolithic communities in Europe, those of the Thessaly Plain, an ideal safe haven from a geographical perspective is found at the head of the Pagasitic Gulf in the Aegean Sea, probably just visible from the village site at Sesklo in this period. In the later Neolithic and Early Bronze Age, villages at Dimini and Pefkakia appear located to enhance maritime contact; indeed, Pefkakia is situated on a peninsula.

Can we say then that right from the start of crop growing in Europe the expectation was that the sea was a prime means of communication? Here we must heed Doumas's (2004) warning not to equate sea travel in antiquity with the pre-defined routes and schedules of modern motorised shipping. Moreover, does this fit into earlier Mesolithic patterns of mobility? Is it at this time, in the establishment of less mobile patterns of inhabitation, that we witness the development of maritime communities; that is, communities that are tied to both the land and sea, that recognise the requirements of the seafarer and provide safe haven? In a detailed study of the evidence from Early Neolithic Greece, Catherine Perlès (2001) finds that the agriculturalists arrived by sea, rooted themselves in the land, ignored previous patterns of Mesolithic exploitation and re-introduced new patterns of long-distance communication by sea. That this occurs earliest in the Mediterranean in the Aegean region is appropriate and expected given the discussion of a sailing nursery above, but this pattern of settlement must have grown as long-distance voyaging developed into the phenomenon that it was in the Bronze Age.

However, before crediting the seafarers of the Aegean Sea with too much agency in relation to the spread of agriculture, we must not forget that Cyprus was perhaps already colonised by agriculturalists as early as 10,000 years ago, perhaps following earlier visits by foragers and hunters (Jones 2005). Crete appears to be settled by farmers at a similar time as southeast Europe. As Broodbank and Strasser (1991) point out in contrast to acculturation models for the spread of agriculture (e.g., Whittle 1996), here it is clear that people deliberately migrated taking the required elements of agri-pastoral subsistence with them. But these are not the earliest island colonisations in the Mediterranean, if we disregard Sicily, which could have been walked to during times of low sea level. In glacial periods, Sardinia, Corsica and the Balearics all appear to have to have hunter and forager populations from about 9000 BC. Although there is no indication of voyaging or further contacts until the introduction of agriculture millennia later, the initial colonisation does indicate the existence of some form of sea craft, and a willingness to go some distance at that time. Early Neolithic evidence of agriculture in Italy comes from sites on the Tavoliere plain of Apulia in the littoral of the Adriatic Coast. There is evidence from these sites of an expansion in the fishing economy with whales now part of the catch. Whittle (1996) thought that this, along with settlements in eastern Sicily, could be added to Crete and Cyprus as examples of transmission of the Neolithic repertoire by sea rather than land.

In the west Mediterranean, the introduction of agriculture is regarded as much more gradual than that which occurred in the east. We know that people had long-held maritime skills in the west, but that the lack of an obvious sailing nursery perhaps slowed developments in seafaring when compared to the Aegean. The slow adoption of agriculture in the west has often been regarded as a possible result of the filtering effect of the islands of Corsica and Sardinia, where the islanders took on parts of Neolithic repertoire at an early date with only sheep/goats and pottery moving further westwards to begin with. As a type of filter between east and west, the islanders then allowed or selected only certain elements to be taken to the islands and lands of the west Mediterranean. On a much broader geographical scale, a similar effect can be proposed for the expansion of agriculturalists into the islands of the Pacific Ocean. I will discuss this effect in Chapter 7. It is also interesting to note that in the Aeolian Islands, the Early Neolithic sites show no evidence of a maritime economy, so much so that Castagnino Berlinghieri (2003) believes the inhabitants were not seafarers and that they had settled the islands by crossing the 25 kilometres from Sicily on rafts (why rafts should be preferred given there is earlier pre-colonisation evidence from Sicily of the exploitation of the obsidian source is not explained by the author). Once on the islands they established an agro-pastoral subsistence base supplemented by occasional hunting, and they also of course enjoyed the obsidian source of Lipari. At first sight this seems odd, as these are relatively small islands, but if this is the scenario to be believed, and the current evidence supports this, could it be that, like the temples of Malta, the obsidian source was the attractor that brought people to them, requiring no risky sea journeys but introducing imported clay and pots which are attested and the necessary variety of people, animals and plants to enable a healthy existence?

Of course, a significant issue that it is not possible to address is the role played by the complete southern seaboard of the Mediterranean defined by North Africa. Research in these areas has yet to indicate much in relation to Mesolithic and Neolithic activity related to islands and areas of the Mediterranean to the north. Castagnino Berlinghieri (2002) has noted that some 4% of Lipari obsidian identified in Neolithic sites beyond the Aeolian Islands is found in Algeria and a similar amount in Tunisia. If, as I am suggesting, that in the Neolithic long-distance and regular contacts are being made by sea, then there can be little doubt that the shores of Africa would have been reached. It is of course completely possible that there were active agents in seafaring from the African continent, too. For islanders such as the Maltese and other southern Europeans living on the arid margins of Europe, there might have been much to attract them to African shores as there was for the Romans many millennia later. In particular it is possible that decent wood, otherwise in short supply for boat building and roofing, could be obtained. Also, the possibility of a North African route for the introduction of agriculture to the western Mediterranean should not be dismissed out of hand.

In a review of approaches to island archaeology in the Mediterranean, John Cherry (2004) asks why, given that we have to accept that no island in this sea is truly remote, does it take so long for people to settle the islands when they have been living on the adjacent foreshores for hundreds of thousands of years, with some of the islands in the Aegean apparently not permanently settled until the late Neolithic or early Bronze Age? His answer is that there must be an element of biogeography affecting choice. That is, the basic resources of the island may not have been suitable for settlement. Put more colloquially, we would say that the islands settled last (or perhaps the ones not permanently settled at all) were the least desirable. This appears to be a logical conclusion, but perhaps the more difficult part of the question he poses to answer is why there is no evidence for the occupation of Mediterranean islands before c. 10,000 BC. Perhaps this is simply an indication of the lack of appropriate seafaring technology. A spur to the development of this seafaring technology is suggested by Cherry (2004: 237) where he reports 'the loss through submergence of important subsistence resources on the extensive, well-watered plains of the late glacial, for example, in the northern Adriatic and off the coast, which may have greatly increased the attractiveness of offshore islands nearby'. In essence it all returns to choice. Yes, the choices may be restricted by environmental parameters, but the choice as to whether or not to build a boat and the choice as to whether or not to colonise an island were choices nevertheless. As was the choice as to how you construed the sense of your new home and to what uses you put the new technology available to you – you may choose to turn the boat upside down, making it into a roof and live under it, not communicating with outsiders, but this is not typical. Instead these choices begin the process of developing maritime communities, on island and mainland.

Christos Doumas (2004: 215) has pointed out that 'permanent settlement on the Aegean islands . . . presupposes considerable development in the means of maritime migration'. This statement is a truism, but how long does that development have to be around before it is needed in this particular process? Doumas goes on to point out that all islands in the Aegean can be seen to have a corresponding part of a bigger land mass whether Greece, Asia Minor or Crete with which the islanders share strong cultural ties; this he calls the *peraia*. Could it not be the case that the people of these *peraia* areas were already using their sophisticated navigation and maritime technologies to lay claim to and exploit these adjacent islands *before* they felt a need to colonise them with permanent settlements? Given the Aegean heritage of seafaring, is it any surprise that in the Bronze

Age the Minoans were able to establish the world's first recorded thalassocracy?

BACK TO MALTA

Malone and Stoddart (2004) maintain that the distinctiveness of the Maltese temples is due to the relative isolation of what they believe to be small islands in the Neolithic world. They find support from Broodbank (2000) in allowing that the islanders had a choice in the way in which they 'exploited' the sea and in this case they decided it would be a barrier rather than a bridge. But if distinctiveness equates to isolation, how then can the distinctive nature of the archaeological remains either side of 2500 BC be assessed? That is, at the end of the Temple Period, there is a clear break in the architecture and other material culture. Metal is imported and the metal artefacts are types typical of southern Europe at this time. Archaeologists have failed to make any connections between the islanders of the Temple Period and those inhabiting the island after 2500 BC, so much so that there have even been claims that the islands must have been completely abandoned (Magro Conti 1999). There is no sea to intervene here, no choice to be made as to whether to use it as bridge or barrier (although how you would convince outsiders of the latter is perhaps a moot point), but there is a dramatic distinctiveness between the material repertoires and no amount of models derived from island biogeography will explain why. The simple point I wish to make is that distinctiveness is not necessarily a product of isolation. Indeed, I would go further and argue that it is the least parsimonious explanation.

Trump (2002) finds that it is clear from interpreting the archae- ological material that the islanders of Malta maintained external contacts during the Temple Period. Obsidian from Lipari and Pantelleria continued to be imported but different quantities of each at different sites may illustrate different patterns of procurement; a similar story might be told for the different types of flint imported at this time. Red ochre, which appears to have been important for temple decoration and in burial rites, continues to be imported as does exotic stone found in the form of miniature axes and pendants. Apart from the obsidian all of the exotics could be derived from Sicily, but all stand as proxy indicators for the use of sea craft in crossing to Malta at this time. Indeed, Pantelleria which in geographical position must be regarded in at least the same degree of difficulty of navigation as Malta has no evidence of permanent settlement and must have been visited for short periods of quarrying (Cazzella 2002). Malone and Stoddart (2004) accept that imports continued, but they argue that the total import is small and smaller in quantity than pre-Temple phases; however, they rather undermine the validity of their argument that we should pay little heed to these exotics as indicators of contact when they state, 'The Maltese islands were at the end of an exchange network, on the edge of the visible world. Exotic exchange products were always relatively modest in number, and subject to exaggeration in terms of their potency, because so easily identified as different' (2004: 100). As I have previously stated, these are merely proxy indicators of sea travel; they are not the *raison d'etre*. Indeed, as discussed above, it is perhaps the distinctive architecture and its exoticness to others from overseas which provide the key to understanding the Neolithic temples of Malta.

If a single cause could be identified for the construction and elaboration of the unique architectural phenomenon of the Neolithic temples of Malta, then isolation and insularity can be ruled out. The Mediterranean in the Neolithic, as in later periods, was a web of seaways fusing maritime communities on islands and continents in fluid and complex social interactions. Robb (2001) has shown convincingly that for all intents and purposes the material repertoire of exchange in the Temple Period is typical of that of the Copper Age in Sicily and southern Italy. He notes that during the Temple Period, there is clear evidence that elsewhere in Europe identity and individuality are transforming societies and although in a very distinct way, the temples of Malta reflect these broader transformations, creating a 'cultural island' of specific identity rather than a physical island cut off from contemporary events in southern Europe (cf. Whittle 1996). Perhaps the key question is why did the people of the Temple Period maintain their Neolithic technology when metalwork became available?

5

Oceania

Pohnpei and the Eastern Carolines

The thousands of islands of Oceania, excluding the island-continent of Australia and the very large island of New Guinea, are regarded by many as the theatre for island archaeology par excellence. We have already discussed in Chapter 2 how Epeli Hau'ofa describes the region as a 'sea of islands'. John Cherry (2004) in reviewing Mediterranean archaeology not only comments on the many models and analogies borrowed from Oceania, but he also wonders whether if this is at all appropriate (cf. Doumas 2004) given that only in the Pacific Ocean do islands have the distance from continental mainland to make the principles of island biogeography worthy of application. This makes sense given that the Galapagos Islands where Charles Darwin first made observations which would be used to establish the principles of island biogeography are located in this ocean. But in the same way that Cherry and others can question the appropriateness of using cases from Oceania in aid of interpretation of island societies in the past of the Mediterranean, we can ask how applicable the principles of island archaeology are to the long history of island usage in Oceania.

ISLAND HISTORIES IN OCEANIA

By the beginning of the last Ice Age 35,000 years ago, New Guinea and Australia had been settled by humans. At the height of the last Ice Age, c. 18,000 years ago, when sea levels were at their lowest due to water being trapped as ice in the polar regions, Australia and New Guinea formed a single land mass, known to Quaternary scientists as Sahul or Greater Australia. At this time the geography of Southeast Asia also looked radically different with the majority of the islands and the South China Sea adding a huge extension of dry land to the continent; this is usually known as Sunda or Sundaland. At all times in the human past and probably for c. 40 million years, the lands that were to make up Sahul have been separated by a sea gap from Sunda and the rest of the Asian continent. This long-term separation allowed the peculiar evolution of marsupial mammals, such as kangaroos, wallabies and wombats in Sahul compared with the placental mammals common elsewhere, a good example of biogeography, what Darwin might have called 'speciation in isolation' at work. At about the same time that Darwin was making his observations in the Galapagos archipelago, a Welshman, Arthur Russell Wallace, was observing the distinctions between animals from Southeast Asia and Australia. But he also found that in the stepping stone islands between the two areas both types of species could be found, creating a fuzzy boundary between the two biogeographical zones which today is know as Wallacea in his honour.

Although, as commented upon in Chapter 3, we can note the presence of *Homo erectus* on the island of Flores, located between Sunda and Sahul, it is hundreds of thousands of years later before there is any further evidence of hominid movement across the sea. This is the settlement of Sahul, which occurs through seaborne transport on current evidence about 60,000 years ago. Evidence of humans arriving on the present-day island of New Guinea currently stands at approximately 40,000 years ago. Irwin (1992) has discussed the two likely routes utilising stepping stone islands that the colonisers of Sahul might have taken. He illustrates that only short sea crossings were required and that in clear visibility land would always be in sight either behind or in front or in both directions. The explorers or settlers on their bamboo rafts, if that is what they were using, would always have a direct visual contact to head for, reducing the risk of getting lost at sea.

Like the earliest colonisers of some of the Mediterranean islands, the settlers of Sahul were gatherer-hunter-fishers who entered, through the use of water-borne technology, new areas to exploit with new animals to hunt. In Sahul, the new settlers found very large and apparently slow animals which were not used to carnivore predators and many have argued became easy prey to the new arrivals (see Flannery 1994). Tales of such easy pickings would surely have prompted further migrations from Southeast Asia if two-way voyaging was possible at this time.

Once these colonisers arrived and settled on the north coast of New Guinea, it was not long before they were using their skills to exploit new terrains. Here they entered the Oceanic island world by making short sea crossings to New Britain and then to New Ireland; this occurred by 35,000 years ago. By about 30,000 years ago, presumably by island hopping using the small islands south of New Ireland, the island of Buka at the northern end of the Solomon Islands archipelago is settled (Spriggs 1997).

Moving east into these islands, as occurs the further into Oceania one explores, principles of island biogeography are supported by a reduction in species diversity as a ratio to distance from mainland. By at least 20,000 years ago, humans begin to upset the model supplied by island biogeography by deliberately introducing species of wild animals from mainland New Guinea to the islands of New Britain and New Ireland.

Peter White (2004) has reviewed the evidence for wild animal translocation to the islands off the coast of New Guinea. He describes various species of large rats which were likely deliberately introduced by humans, but of specific note is Northern Common Cuscus (*Phalanger orientalis*), which appears in the archaeology of southern New Ireland 20,000 years ago. These animals, when full grown, average approximately 2 kilograms in weight and in recent times have been hunted for food. White (2004: 157) believes that translocation of such animals 'implies a long-term intention with a planned outcome rather than a series of accidents' and goes on to suggest that such wild animal introductions provided more than a supplement to the food base, but various body parts would be used for 'decoration, dress, as tools, and in ceremonies' (2004: 159). Along with animals, at around the same time, and perhaps 10,000 years before the obsidian from Melos in the Mediterranean is being exploited by sea, obsidian from a source at Mopir in New Britain is being transported across the sea to New Ireland.

Cuscus, which is a type of possum, is also introduced to the island of Manus in the Admiralties group, northwest of New Ireland, by about 12,000 years ago. Although these animal translocations provide early human evidence for spoiling simple island biogeographical profiles and also give useful proxy evidence of inter-island water-borne transport, the archaeology of Manus also provides us with evidence of a significant event in the history of seafaring. Present evidence indicates that humans colonised Manus prior to 13,000 years ago and in so doing the settlers had to sail beyond sight of land in any direction. Indeed, a 'blind' voyage of some 60 to 90 kilometres was required in a 230-kilometre trip between the closest island, New Hanover, and Manus (Spriggs 1997). This is the earliest evidence of such a voyage, which is unlikely to be an accident as it produced a viable population of humans and was repeated to introduce the Cuscus. It may be no exaggeration to compare placing humans on the moon with the 'giant leap' this represents (cf. Finney 1992).

The islands of New Britain, New Ireland and New Hanover form the Bismarck Archipelago and along with part of the New Guinea mainland and the Admiralties including Manus define the area of the Bismarck Sea. As discussed in Chapter 3, this is the area defined by Geoff Irwin (1992) as a possible sailing nursery. Although we must be careful not to overstate the magnitude of inter-island mobility in the Late Pleistocene of the region (cf. Bellwood 1997b), the evidence as it currently stands obviously indicates a confidence in using sea transport, which stands the people of the region in good stead for further developments in maritime technology and utilisation.

These developments do not occur for millennia, but when they do they do at a remarkable pace. In a period of approximately 500 years beginning some 3500–3300 years ago, people using a distinctive pottery called Lapita settled on all of the island groups from the Bismarck Archipelago east as far as the West Polynesian islands of Samoa and Tonga, a distance of some 5500 kilometres and requiring direct sea crossings of as much as 900 kilometres in distance (Kirch 2000). Like the settlers of the majority of the Mediterranean islands, these people were agriculturalists and they took with them viable populations of plants and animals, transforming the islands on arrival through a 'transported landscape', in order to subsist.

A transported landscape is the conveyance of most, if not all, subsistence items found in the repertoire of the colonists' home island. In the case of island colonisation, although some animal species may die, and certain crops fail, at least elements of the package should flourish and allow a diverse subsistence base to be established. A corollary of this is that it may be possible to trace the origin of a settler community by the landscape they appear to have transported with them.

In general, the colonisers of the islands of Oceania after 3300 years ago took with them all or some of the items from an available suite for subsistence of dog, pig, chicken, rat, taro, yam and breadfruit. Rats are included here as their role as a fast-breeding, self-feeding source of food for human consumption has often been under-rated; they are commonly written off as stowaways which crept onto ocean-going sea craft under the cover of darkness (cf. White, Clark and Bedford 2000). The full complement of subsistence species is common in islands closest to New Guinea, but appears to dwindle with distance from source (Kirch 1984). This may be due to death of a species during a voyage or unsuccessful transplantation, but may also indicate the presence of filter effect as mentioned in the previous chapter. For example, as there is no evidence of pigs in the pre-European past of New Caledonia, it may be because this element of the transported landscape package was not allowed to be taken from Vanuatu, creating a filtering effect.

By necessity, the settlers of new islands, initially living on the reefs, actively set about altering the landscape in order to create the conditions they perceived as suitable for settlement and subsistence. Their aim was to alter the very nature of the landscape, by cutting down native vegetation so as to cause erosion and thereby lay the foundations for their subsistence systems, in a landscape transported as much by mind as by sea craft. This approach to the landscape by the initial settlers would be responsible for creating conditions of high sediment transport and the progradation of the shoreline onto the reef flats, possibly underneath stilt house settlements. This was an application of their habitual experience of island landscape alteration, an experience attested at Lapita pottery sites in Melanesia.

Over the next two millennia, virtually all of the inhabitable islands, including Hawaii and Aotearoa/New Zealand, were settled. I will return to this below, but first we must head to the tropical northwest Pacific, where other significant events of the maritime past were occurring.

MICRONESIA

The islands of the western Pacific Ocean north of the equator are usually labelled Micronesia as part of the tripartite division of Oceania

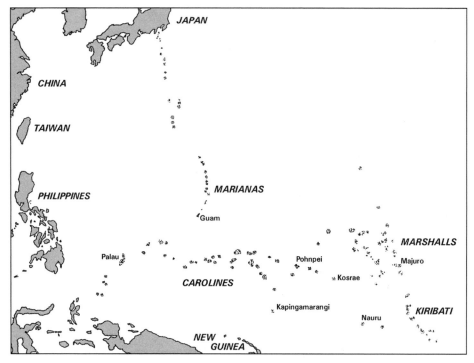

9. Map of the Western Pacific (drafted by author)

developed in the first half of the eighteenth century (Figure 9). These divisions are not without their problems (see Thomas 1989; Rainbird 2003) and so far in this chapter I have been, for the most part, discussing the histories of islands in Melanesia where an expansion of settlement of previously uninhabited islands begins some 3300 years ago. In Micronesia, the tropical northwest Pacific, settlement of the distant archipelagos of the Marianas and Palau appears to begin earlier, probably by 3500 years ago and possibly as early as 4500 years ago (Rainbird 2004).

What we find, based on present understanding, is that the Marianas are first settled at the same time as, or a few centuries prior, the emergence of Lapita pottery-using communities in the Bismarck Archipelago. Unlike the Lapita evidence, however, the Marianas material provides unequivocal evidence for the deliberate migration of pottery-using people into Oceania. These people, who were presumably accomplished sailors in sophisticated sea craft, may have travelled across the open sea a straight-line distance of at least 1800 kilometres. All of the archaeological and linguistic evidence points to this being a colonising expedition derived from Southeast Asia. It would indicate a separate locale for maritime innovations, perhaps in the South China Sea as Peter Bellwood (1997b) has proposed. Bellwood (1997a) also gives a strong indication of the motivations of such developments in providing a figure of some 2.2 million square kilometres of land lost in Sunda to the rising seas of the Early Holocene.

The prevailing winds in this region are east and northeast (Karolle 1993: Figure 30), which means that the supposed direction of colonisation from the Philippines fits into the model proposed by Irwin (1992). In Irwin's model, the safest strategy for exploration and colonisation is to sail against the direction of the prevailing wind, which reduces risk, as explorers are more able to return home down-wind if no landfall is made. Direct colonisation of the Marianas or Palau (depending on which happened first) in this manner would constitute the longest sea crossing undertaken by that time in human history. However, we should be aware of the possibility that we are not dealing with a single colonisation event for each group of islands.

The alternative, and on current evidence, less likely model for the colonisation for western Micronesia, is a movement of people through the Bird's Head of New Guinea and passing northward via the tiny southwest islands of Tochobei (Tobi), Pulo Anna and Sonsorol, as stepping stones to Palau and the Mariana Islands. The most recent dates for early settlement of Palau places it before that of the Marianas in the chronology of human settlement so would fit this model and reduce the need for the extremely long sea voyage. In an analysis of accessibility and relative isolation, Geoff Irwin (2000: 397) finds:

If [the Marianas] had been settled directly from Island Southeast Asia, then this would have been a very long and difficult offshore voyage. The accessibility of the Marianas directly from the Philippines . . . means that it approaches in difficulty voyages made into the margins of East Polynesia, at a much later time in prehistory. Therefore it may be deemed more likely that settlement of the Marianas followed an easier but indirect route *via* Palau, then to Yap, and on to Guam – which is the southernmost of the Marianas.

So, in Irwin's assessment, the long voyage model of colonisation is not impossible; it just does not happen in Oceania until several centuries later. However, it might be useful to note here that Atholl Anderson (2000) has proposed that the margins of eastern Polynesia were not settled until Micronesian seafaring technology was introduced to Polynesia. Could it be, then, that differences in developments at the two (or more) sailing nursery locales in the west of Oceania did not merge until meetings in western Polynesia, probably less than 2000 years ago? And this meeting of traditions allowed the islanders of Polynesia to complete the settlement of Oceania and likely continuing voyaging as far as the Americas. Certainly the sweet potato was derived from South America at least 1000 years ago, becoming a staple of subsistence across much of Oceania (Hather and Kirch 1991). It has been proposed that there is much from archaeology and ethnography to indicate the presence of Polynesians in southern California some 1600 to 1200 years ago (Jones and Klar 2005). That the islanders of Oceania are the likely prime movers in regard to mobility and contact is an expectation based on their clear achievements in the sea-borne exploration and colonisation of the Pacific Ocean.

In recent times, the region of Micronesia has been regarded as a 'backwater' of Pacific archaeology (Davidson 1988), a distinct area separate from the main west to east flow of migration and oceanic cultural development, such as notions of the evolution of the Polynesian chiefdoms (Kirch 1984). However, as noted above, developments in Micronesia, specifically those related to maritime achievements, may have had a more significant role than previously recognised, perhaps

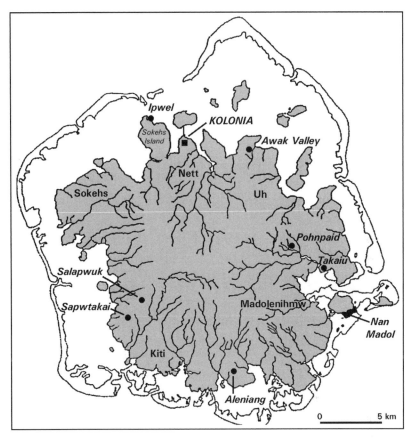

10. Map of Pohnpei, Federated States of Micronesia (drafted by author)

closer to that envisaged by Te Rangi Hiroa in *Vikings of the Sunrise*, where the route to Polynesia 'leads through Yap, Palau, and the Caroline Islands; then it branches, one line leading northeast through the Marshall Islands toward Hawaii, and one going southeast through the Gilbert and Phnix Islands to enter Polynesia north of Samoa' (Buck 1938: 45).

It is the Caroline Islands I wish to turn to now, and in particular the island of Pohnpei (formerly Ponape) located in the eastern end of this chain of islands (Figure 10). It might be argued from an island archaeology perspective that Pohnpei shares many similarities with the far-distant Maltese archipelago. With an area of 330 square kilometres it is of a similar size to Malta and Gozo, which have a combined area of 303 square kilometres. Although Pohnpei is big in its regional context, it is the third largest of the islands in the region, and by far the largest of the eastern Carolines, whereas Malta is regarded as a small island. Pohnpei is mountainous and consequently annual rainfall is extremely high, allowing for large rivers and dense vegetation. The mountains reach an elevation of 790 metres and support cloud forest; Malta is relatively flat with low rainfall and no rivers. The majority of Pohnpei is surrounded by a barrier reef, creating a large lagoon with several smaller islands. Malta has no lagoon. The geology of Pohnpei is igneous basalt compared to the sedimentary limestone of Malta. The distance to the nearest mainland is thousands of kilometres for Pohnpei compared to the relatively miniscule 80 kilometres from Malta to Sicily. Indeed, Malta's 300 kilometres to North Africa appears small when considering the distances involved in the geography of Pohnpei. Unlike Malta, there was little in the way of local resources to attract visitors to Pohnpei prior to settlement by agriculturalists. The initial colonists who arrived between 2500 and 2000 years ago brought with them the plants and animals they required for subsistence purposes, beyond what the sea could provide. It is possible that full colonisation only occurred once the island was seeded and subsistence plants established (Rainbird 2004).

In comparison, however, both islands have examples of ancient monumental architecture regarded as unique to their specific locales. On Pohnpei the most intensively explored example is at Nan Madol, but other examples are found across the island. The complex of Nan Madol is located on the tidal fringing reef of a small island which itself is located on the fringing reef of the main island proper. The stone architecture consists of walls up to 7 metres in height, a large breakwater, mortuary structures, tunnels and canals. The canals are defined by ninety-two islets constructed with basalt walls and in-filled with coral rubble; the architectural embellishments are constructed on these islets.

Construction of the complex appears to begin around 1500 years ago and it may be no accident that the site chosen was one previously used by the earliest settlers of the island, perhaps living in stilt houses on the fringing reef. A strong association with the ancestors appears to be maintained throughout the history of the site (Rainbird 1999b). The last phase of new stone building may have been completed about 800 years ago. The tidal canals have earned the appellation for Nan Madol of the 'Venice of the Pacific'. The key questions of the origins, use and possible demise of Nan Madol are not easily answered.

Oral histories tell us that Nan Madol was constructed for the *Saudeleurs*, an evil dictatorship who are reputed to have ruled Pohnpei through a harsh regime that involved exacting massive tribute from the island population. They were all seeing over the island, which they could view by peering into a pool on one of the Nan Madol islets. Terrible retribution would follow any transgression of their law. Isohkelekel, returning from overseas, is the man reputed to have freed Pohnpeians from this awful regime by defeating the last of the *Saudeleur* dynasty.

Cultural anthropologist Glenn Petersen (1990b) has shown convincingly in the Pohnpei context how such stories are used as metaphors for political purposes and, as such, has warned archaeologists not to take them literally but rather rely on the archaeological evidence for constructing interpretations of past times. The archaeological evidence is derived, for the most part, from work independently instigated and directed by William Ayres and Steve Athens (for references see review in Rainbird 2004). Their excavations and surveys have found evidence of multiple uses including domestic residences, rituals and mortuary functions for various islets. In terms of the spatial distribution of these functions, I have noted (Rainbird 1999b, 2004, 2006) the seaward distribution of the mortuary islets, which includes the outer length of the breakwater. Identification of tombs in this area of the site includes the recovery of human skeletal remains representing open access to all ages and sexes, indicating ascribed rather than achieved status for inclusion. Grave goods include numerous shell beads, shell adzes and broken representations of pearl shell fishing lures. These grave goods, I argue, are deliberately referencing the sea in the form of the material of their manufacture, but more so with the latter, which represents the memory of former activities at sea. Trolling, the type of fishing using lures, may no longer have been practised at the time of deposition (see Rainbird in press). Not only do these tombs likely represent some of the later constructions at the site, perhaps indicating a change in attitude towards ancestral remains, but their location and contents also indicate a new association with the sea and the outside world which the sea may symbolise.

Whereas on Malta it is the axes of the monumental temples which appear to reference the direction of the ancestral beginnings and the outside world on Pohnpei, at Nan Madol it appears that the construction of the tombs at the very edge of reef, where it drops off rapidly to meet deep water, may be doing the same thing. At Nan Madol, the most spectacular architecture, the sweeping basalt walls of Nan Douwas, contains a series of tombs and is located adjacent to a break in the sea wall (Figure 11). This break in the sea wall would allow passage, at high tide, for sea craft coming from deep sea; indeed, it is often used to bring visitors to the site in the present day. It is, I suggest, no accident that visitors arriving from the open sea find themselves immediately confronted by the most monumental architecture and symbols of the ancestors. Could it be, as I have proposed for the temples of Malta, that the monumental architecture here works as an attractor to bring people from elsewhere to the island? And if so, is there something peculiar about an island which leads to such apparently unique developments?

Let us start by looking at the first question asked. For Malta we know through the presence of exotic materials that communication with the outside world was continuing through the temple building period. I proposed that the Maltese would not need to be sailors themselves as the monumental architecture, and rites performed there, would be enough to attract outsiders and maintain the desired influx of people and things. For Pohnpei, given the notoriety of the effectiveness of traditional maritime skills accredited to the Caroline Islanders (see Chapter 2), it is odd that earliest records made by European visitors indicate that the Pohnpeians do not possess

11. Nan Douwas, Nan Madol, Pohnpei. This is the mortuary islet directly adjacent to the deep water entrance to the complex (source author, 1997)

ocean-going sailing vessels and that they do not venture beyond the barrier reef in water craft. This would account for the apparent lack of trolling using lures alluded to above. There is no environmental reason why, at some time after colonising the island, the Pohnpeians needed to stop building large sea craft. Unlike their neighbours on the atolls, they had appropriate materials in abundance. It is quite possible then that the relatively resource-rich islanders of Pohnpei were able to put their energies into the goodly works for the ancestors in monumental construction safe in the knowledge that nearby atoll dwellers required their island as a *peraia*, to borrow the term used by Doumas to describe established mainland contacts (see Chapter 4). Additionally, the works themselves would bring fame and visitors from further asea. So successful was this that, at a later date, the neighbouring high islanders of Kosrae, some 550 kilometres to the east of Nan Madol, built their own version.

Is this then purely an island phenomenon? Are we witnessing here the same cultural elaboration and exaggerated development that Evans claimed for Malta (and Easter Island)? Well, no, because Evans's model was based on relative isolation, whereas the argument here is that these monuments were built with the expectation that visitors would come. These are not souvenirs, though; they are not meaningless in their own context, and they have other internal roles for which local explanations can be made. Can the *moai*, the great carved stone heads and torsos of Rapa Nui (Easter Island), be explained similarly? If we reject the orthodox models of the *moai* representing competition leading to resource depletion (cf. Rainbird 2002a), then the notoriety that these have gained in the modern world may have been an intention of earlier designs. Why should the seven wonders of the ancient world be restricted to the broader classical world area? But Evans aside, is this a peculiar island phenomenon? The answer has to be no again. Monumental constructions, beyond functional requirements, are witnessed elsewhere. For example, two from Egypt, the Pharos of Alexandria and the Pyramids, neither were required to be constructed in the ways they were (or apparently were in regard to the Pharos) in order to meet the requirements of their basic functions.

The question we can ask specifically of the Pohnpei evidence is did it work? That is, is there archaeological evidence to show that people continued to visit the island?

The first direct evidence comes from the tombs themselves. Here the pearl shell for the trolling lure is likely imported. We know from ethnographic sources that the Caroline Islanders could be very selective in regards to where shells for ornaments and fishing gear were sourced. Robert Gillett (1987) in his study of tuna fishing amongst the Satawal islanders found that pearl shell from Chuuk Lagoon was highly prized for manufacturing into lures as the vivid colours were described as 'like a rainbow'. Mark Berg (1992), in discussing the *sawei* exchange system of the central and western Carolines, has argued convincingly that one of the most valuable items of tribute was small *Spondylus* shell beads, known as *gau*, that came from specific locations, namely, Eauripik Atoll, Udot Island in Chuuk Lagoon, and Etal Atoll in the Mortlocks group, southeast of Chuuk.

The second and third pieces of archaeological evidence are also related to shell, but this time in regard to the species used for the manufacture of adzes and a new type of adze. An adze manufactured by splitting and sharpening the *Terebra* bivalve, although common in Palau from an early date, becomes a common type across the whole of the Caroline Islands after about 1000 years ago. While dating it to a few centuries later, John Craib (nd) has argued for the widespread adoption of the beaked adze, fabricated from the hinge of the giant *Terebra* clam, which is another distinctive style of adze and not previously known in the Carolines, but with a distribution over a wide area of the southwest Pacific.

A fourth indicator, although poorly dated, relates to rock-art. Pohnpaid is a complex of engraved rocks and boulders situated above the Lehdau River in the Sapwalap village area of Madolenihmw, in the same district as Nan Madol in the south east of Pohnpei Island. A detailed recording of the engravings (petroglyphs) identified over 750 individual motifs. The majority of the motifs consist of a number of repeated forms, which included human foot and hand prints, human figures (anthropomorphs), fish, hooks, dots and circles. An especially interesting find was the presence of enveloped crosses, a type previously known only in Melanesia (both painted and engraved), and suggestive of wider communication and contact, but presently undated (Rainbird and Wilson 2002).

Also undated, but another indicator of contact, is the introduction of *kava* into the eastern Carolines, as it is highly likely that its immediate origins were in western Polynesia. The *Piper methysticum* plant, which is used on various islands across Oceania to prepare the mildly narcotic drink *kava*, is found in Pohnpei as *sakau*. In Pohnpei, it is prepared by pounding the roots on basalt slabs, adding water and straining the liquid out of the resulting mulch by squeezing it through straps of hibiscus bark. Although common and available in bars in the present day, its use in contemporary events and as recorded ethnographically follows strict protocol. Utilising a variety of techniques, including botanic, genetic and chemical evidence, northern Vanuatu has been identified as the most likely area for the domestication and initial dispersal of *P. methysticum* (Lebot 1991; Lebot, Merlin and Lindstrom 1992). Pounding stones for the preparation of *sakau* is a ubiquitous feature of archaeological sites on Pohnpei, and it appears that consuming this narcotic drink is probably an old practice, but one introduced through contact with Polynesians (Crowley 1994).

In celebrating their ancestors and attracting visitors, the apparent lack of long-distance sea craft on Pohnpei, at the time of earliest European reporting, may not be so odd. The effort represented in the goodly works at these places acted as attractors. Stories collected from Ulithi Atoll, far to the west, recount visits to Pohnpei and Nan Madol. People came from the sea and Pohnpeians learnt to control visitors and extract what they required from them. Identification of themes in Pohnpeian oral history finds that visitors were to be expected. One consistent aspect amongst the variety of stories related to the initial discovery, construction and settlement of Pohnpei is the continuing introduction of people and things from the outside. This theme of foreign introduction and incorporation is not without a certain ambivalence, but Petersen (1990a: 12) finds that '[t]he emphasis given by these early tales to Pohnpei's reliance on the outer world resonates in modern Pohnpei. The people see interaction with the rest of the world as fundamental to their own existence.'

But if the Pohnpeians themselves were not the active agents of interaction, in that they did not actively engage in inter-island voyaging, then who did? The Carolines form a string of islands running 3000 kilometres between the Palau Archipelago in the west and the high igneous peaks of Kosrae in the east; between these are the only other high island groups of Chuuk Lagoon and Pohnpei. Here we need to consider the role of the atoll dwellers, the people of the low islands, which make up the vast majority of the islands of the Carolines and all of the Marshall Islanders and Kiribati (formerly the Gilbert Islands) to the east and southeast of Pohnpei. We have already seen in Chapter 3 that most of what is known about traditional Oceanic voyaging is derived from the navigators of the central Carolinian atolls.

Geologically speaking, most of the atolls in this region are relatively young and it is not clear that all were present, or at the least inhabitable, at 2000 years ago when the remaining high islands were colonised. Some, though, have produced dates of equivalent antiquity and there is certainly no reason to suppose that any of the currently inhabited atolls were not available to human settlement 1000 years ago.

Images of atolls often capture the imagination by providing the picture postcard version of an archetypal desert island of sand, palms and an azure blue lagoon. These tropical blues contrast with the deep and dark blues that lap, or crash, at the outside of the reef. Ecologically, atolls have often been regarded as marginal environments for human populations, having a small land area, poor coralline soils and vulnerability to extreme environmental events such as typhoons. However, Rosalind Hunter-Anderson and Yigal Zan (1996) have collated evidence from a number of researchers that challenges the notion of atolls as impoverished environments in terms of food production. Typically, in Micronesia, atoll islands (or islets) have a central taro patch that has been mulched and developed over centuries, and breadfruit and coconut trees circle this. It is also the case, and here seafaring ability was of paramount importance, that the Carolinian atoll islanders were involved in a number of small-scale exchange systems, at inter-island or intra-atoll scale, that, amongst other things, mutually benefited the participants at times of localized food shortage (Hage and Harary 1991).

It also should be noted that inter-community interaction was not always friendly and for the sharing of aid, as the historical reports of fighting between atoll communities attest, including between atoll dwellers of widely separated island groups (Spennemann 2005). However, the network of exchange could also be extensive and of undoubted benefit. For example, in the case of the widely reported *sawei* tribute system, the people of the atolls were subordinate to the people of the Gagil area of the high island of Yap, within the fictive idiom of a 'parent–child' relationship. Whenever requested by the Yapese 'parents', the outer islanders were required to sail westwards, starting almost as far as Chuuk Lagoon some 1000 kilometres away, collecting others on the way, until the final fleet sailed from Mogmog in Ulithi Atoll closest to Yap. Due to restrictions placed on the movement of Carolinians in the German and Japanese colonial periods (1898 to 1945), the system, known from oral history, was not ethnographically recorded and details are at times contradictory. It appears, however, that the tribute was paid approximately every three years. The Outer Islanders gave gifts, either directly to the chief of Gatchepar village, or to particular Gagil people who were notionally regarded as 'owners' of particular atolls or parts of them. The gifts included fibre skirts and loincloths, shell valuables, sennit twine, coconut- and turtle-shell belts, pandanus leaf mats and coconut oil. In return, the Yapese gave their 'children' ceramic pots, wood for canoe building, red-earth pigment, turmeric, *Tridacna* clamshells and a variety of foodstuffs. This system allowed the atoll dwellers to augment their resource base. Once again we might say this is an example of Yap acting as the *peraia* to these atoll islanders.

The atoll dwellers had the skill and requirement to act as the agents of communication in Micronesia. It is also clear that linguistic boundaries were no barrier with the *sawei* system, as an example in linking the Chuukic speakers of the atolls with the non-mutually intelligible Yapese speakers of the high island. As noted in Chapter 3, maritime communities are adept at developing means of communication across linguistic boundaries, including the development of a *patois*. Although no such *patois* is known from the Carolines, there is no reason to believe that the islanders in the region did not possess the ability to communicate in their own language and those of a number of their immediate neighbours.

The evidence for these widespread seaways is slowly starting to amount to significant material confirmation of widespread contact and communication in Micronesia prior to Magellan's arrival in Guam in AD 1521. It is, I propose, this milieu of local seaways and social networks across fluid boundaries into which the Europeans stumbled. We have seen that inter-island voyaging has a long history in Oceania, but how does the scenario developed here for Micronesia compare to that other major group of inhabited islands in remote Oceania, Polynesia?

POLYNESIA

Early European accounts of Polynesia have recently been characterised as consistent in reporting no evidence of inter-archipelago voyaging at this time, and an expression of surprise as to how these people managed to settle these islands in the first place (e.g., Anderson 2003; Rolett 2002). This is at odds with earlier publications which provided a great deal to contradict this view. For example, Greg Dening (1972), in a response to Andrew Sharp's (1963) 'pessimistic' theory that proposed the settlement of the Polynesian islands by accidental drift voyaging, collated historical references pertaining to deliberate inter-island voyaging in Polynesia. Examining ship's logs, seamen's journals and missionary accounts of early encounters with Pacific islanders, Dening finds 'positive evidence for Polynesian deliberate voyages' (1972: 125). The patterns he identifies in the historical accounts suggest regions of intense contact, namely: the Society-Tuamotu area; Tonga-Samoa; Tonga-Fiji; Tonga-Rotuma; and more local intra-group interaction in the Societies and Southern Cook Islands. These records of regular inter-archipelagic contacts need to be considered within terms of the relativity of distance, that is, scale, when defining voyaging events. Dening (1972) points out that many of the voyages even within archipelagos, such as the Society Islands, may require passages at open sea lasting over six days and illustrating the ability of Pacific islanders historically to navigate over a long duration which would not be problematic to extend for longer journeys.

It is from the Society Islands that we gain one of the best historical insights into the navigational ability of Polynesians in the period of European contact. During Cook's second voyage (1772–1775), the Tahitian navigator Tupaia provided geographical information which was collated by Johann Reinhold Forster (1996 [1778]: 303–318), who was a naturalist on the expedition. For the most part derived from the information gained from Tupaia, Forster was able to produce a list of the names of eighty-three islands known to the Tahitians at this time, along with a rudimentary chart of their geographical location. Forster (1996: 318) was so impressed by the force of the information he compiled that he stated:

> The foregoing account of the many islands mentioned by Tupaya [sic] is sufficient to prove that the inhabitants of the islands in the South Sea have made very considerable navigators in their slight and weak canoes; navigations which many Europeans would think impossible to be performed, upon a careful view of the vessels themselves, their rigging, sails, &c. &c. also the provisions of the climate.

However, the historical sources, although providing a hint to past practices, cannot on their own provide an insight into past Pacific islander sailing patterns. We must turn to archaeological sources for an indication of these past patterns. Having said this, though, the basic underlying and undeniable fact is that people hailing from small-scale Neolithic societies found and successfully settled (and occasionally abandoned) what in the present day are regarded as some of the most remote and isolated pieces of land in the world. How they achieved this and at what time are matters that remain available for debate.

Irwin's (1992) model of exploration against the wind over a wide front, along with continuous attempts by the islanders to find new land, has been questioned by Anderson (2000, 2003). Anderson finds three assumptions open to critique: (1) the assumed abilities of ancient craft, (2) the need for a wide exploratory corridor and (3) the chronological basis for assuming continuous exploration. His alternative views on these points provide a rather more parsimonious account:

1. He finds that the evidence from experimental voyaging is questionable, especially given the sailing rig and materials likely available to Polynesian seafarers as these do not behave as well as the modern materials usually used on experimental craft. Sailing in traditional craft would then be much more difficult than generally assumed.

2. According to Anderson the 'grain of the islands' beyond New Guinea, both in their location and shape of their archipelagos, is one that has an orientation of northwest to southeast. By travelling southeast, the majority of the islands of central and eastern Polynesia would be discovered, and this would quickly be recognised, meaning the direction of exploration would be much narrower and equally successful, with much less effort, than in the broad front model proposed by Irwin. The discovery of Hawaii and Aotearoa/New Zealand would then be possible by sailing at right angles to the axis of discovery.

3. Anderson, an advocate of chronometric hygiene, is of the view that a short chronology is supported by reliable radiocarbon dates for first human settlement in central and eastern Polynesia. Following the settlement of Fiji-Tonga-Samoa by Lapita pottery

users 2800 years ago, there is a gap of approximately 1700 years before a renewed period of exploration resulting in rapid colonisation of all of remaining Polynesia except Aotearoa/New Zealand, which was settled a couple centuries later still. This certainly required voyaging over distances at a different order of scale compared with that which had been required to settle west Polynesia (a minimum of 900 kilometres from Vanuatu to Fiji), Mangareva to Rapa Nui (Easter Island) 2300 kilometres, the Marquesas to Hawaii being 3200 kilometres, although a halfway stop could have been had at Fanning Island. Tahiti to Aotearoa/New Zealand was a similar order of magnitude, but once again a stop could have been taken at the Kermadecs.

Anderson's punctuate model of colonisation contrasts with the continuous model favoured by Irwin and others (e.g., Kirch 2000), and need not detain us here. However, as previously mentioned, Anderson thinks that it may have been maritime technological innovations introduced from Micronesia which provided improvements required to expand the distances explored.

Once Polynesia was inhabited, it is clear that contacts were maintained between the island communities. Marshall Weisler (1998) in reviewing the evidence from the geochemical sourcing of basalt adzes, which appear to have been exchanged over long distances, concludes that routine voyages could be up to 1750 kilometres in distance. Barry Rolett (2002) regards the Society Islands as a hub for these regular voyages, with occasional two-way voyages beyond this sphere of interaction to Hawaii, Rapa Nui and Aotearoa/New Zealand. Both Weisler and Rolett find that the archaeological evidence for inter-archipelago contacts is significantly less after c. AD 1450, and this may explain the historical accounts indicating little long-distance voyaging. Why this should have occurred is a matter of much speculation. According to Rolett the lessening in contacts could have been due to a number of combined factors such as the reduction through deforestation of appropriate trees for sea craft manufacture, the establishment of settled communities in need of less things from external sources to maintain a healthy population, or a rise in warfare in the hub group of the Societies and a similar development in the Marquesas, each serious enough to have consequences for voyaging.

FUSION

Oceanic settlement by its very nature is fusion. Colonialism brought with it displacement and relocation for many islanders, leaving many gaps in historical records. The movement of people across the fluid boundaries provided by the ocean had a long history and, as maritime communities became established, relationships changed. Internal developments could have significant external consequences across the seaways, altering directionality. When Europeans arrived, they too arrived by sea and a communication system which was in a perpetual state of flux became fossilized by record and colonial imperative.

We surely cannot continue to use the island as microcosm as a means to understanding the long-term history in the islands of Oceania. Rather, fusion and fluidity, with the necessity of considering flux in political and social allegiances, allied with environmental change provide the opportunity for a different way of thinking about the Pacific past – one that is not restricted to limited locales but recognises that the world of these islanders stretched far beyond the horizon. Returning to Pohnpei, interaction with the outside world may indeed have been fundamental to the people of this island in the past. The Pohnpeians had ancestors and goodly works on display. Even then, the Pohnpeians jealously maintain the ability to control this interaction and reserve the right to make the island invisible – hidden in a great mass of clouds – to any undesirables sailing past it on the open seas (Petersen 1990a).

The Baltic

Gotland

In this chapter, we move to more northerly latitudes and focus on the island of Gotland located in the Baltic Sea (Figure 12). Gotland is not only rich in the archaeology of the prehistoric past but also provides an excellent example of how palaeoenvironmental change can alter the status of the designation of the land form. Although much larger in size than Malta or Pohnpei, it is not part of a sea of islands; it is an island in the middle with mainland to be found in all directions, a peculiar situation that lends an appeal to the island as a hub for maritime communication in the Baltic.

■ GOTLAND

Gotland, part of modern-day Sweden, is located 80 kilometres east of the mainland. The nearest land is the Swedish

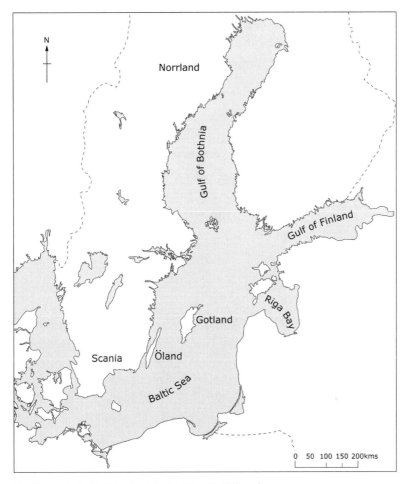

12. Map of the Baltic Sea (drafted by H. Wilson)

island of Öland which is 50 kilometres distant. East from Gotland, it is 140 kilometres to Latvia, south is 220 kilometres to Poland and Finland is 280 kilometres to the north. There is no inter-visibity between Gotland and any neighbouring land. It is a plateau-like island reaching elevations of little higher than 80 metres and, like Malta, is composed of limestone bedrock. In Oceanic terms, it is a raised limestone island. Gotland consists of two main islands (Gotland and Fårö) with some small outliers amounting to a total land area of 3140 square kilometres (Figure 13). Things have not always been this way. At various times in the past,

13. Map of Gotland (drafted by H. Wilson)

the island has been covered by thick ice or consisted of a group of smaller islands emerging from the waters of the Baltic.

People arrived on the islands, which for ease are normally grouped together and called Gotland, in the early Mesolithic, soon after the ice had retreated at the beginning of the Holocene. At this time ice continued to retreat northwards, and the land of southern Scandinavia relieved of the weight rose and blocked the link from the Atlantic to the Yoldia Sea (in the Baltic basin), thus removing the saline input and creating a body of freshwater known as the Ancylus Lake. Gotland was certainly an island at this time and raised coastal ridges (between 20 and 45 metres above sea level) on the island containing the shells of a freshwater gastropod, *Ancylus fluviatalis*, attest to this (Olsson and Öhrman 1996: 19–20). At about 8000 years ago, the dry land which joined present-day southern Sweden and Denmark and divided freshwater lake from saltwater ocean was severed again and the Litorina Sea was formed, turning the water from fresh to brackish, which has continued as the Baltic Sea of the present day.

MESOLITHIC GOTLAND

The earliest sites for human habitation date to the Ancylus Lake period; the earliest known site is Stora Förvar, a sea cave on the off-shore island of Stora Karlsö, some 8 kilometres west of Gotland proper. The cave was extensively excavated in the late nineteenth century and was not fully published by the excavators, but some of the material has subsequently been reanalysed and contextualised by Christian Lindqvist and Göran Possnert (1997, 1999). Stora Förvar has demonstrated use over a long period of time, starting at before 9000 years ago based on radiocarbon dates. There is evidence of substantial Mesolithic occupation with 1.2 metres of deposits covered by a further metre of Neolithic period deposits. Detailed reanalysis has provided an osteoarchaeological assessment of part of the site, indicating the remains of at least ten humans, and masses of faunal remains, including approximately 16,000 identified bones from the Mesolithic layer. The humans represent all ages from baby to adult and both sexes, suggesting evidence of actual and pre-meditated colonisation rather than a hunting party or accidental stranding.

The animal remains also indicate slaughter in all seasons of the year with salmon and pike caught in the summer, ringed seals in the late summer and autumn, grey seal cubs in the winter and spring, and the taking of an occasional migratory aquatic bird along with hare in the late autumn, winter and early spring (Lindqvist and Possnert 1997).

The two species of seal, ringed and grey, must have migrated to the Baltic during the Yoldia Sea phase and successfully adapted to the freshwater of the Ancylus Lake. Three sites on Gotland proper also date to the early Mesolithic. At Strå kalkbrott and Svalings artefacts and bones, including seal and possibly a fragment of human cranium at Svalings, were recovered from below marine-derived gravels of the Litorina Sea. At Gisslause, the assemblage consisting of many flint and bone artefacts and bones from hare, grey seal, rudd, pike and roach have also been identified. There had been earlier claims from limited evidence of elk, deer, horse and wild boar dating to the Mesolithic on Gotland. Lindqvist and Possnert (1997) convincingly show that these are either poorly provenanced, badly dated or were special items imported from the mainland, such as the cases of the two red deer antler tips in an early Mesolithic grave at Stora Bjärs and a harpoon, possibly Mesolithic, made from red deer antler and found at Stora Förvar. The only evidence for terrestrial mammals at first settlement comes from the arctic (forest, mountain) hare (*Lepus timidus*), leading Lindqvist and Possnert (1999: 69) to opine that the first colonisers, having been used to hunting deer and wild boar on the mainland, 'probably were quite surprised when they realized that this large island – in spite of a lush vegetation and plenty of fresh water – entirely lacked large terrestrial game.' This, they think, also explains the lack of formal geometric microliths typical on the mainland, as a different type of hunting kit was required for the mainly water-based resources of the island.

Many previous commentators (e.g., see Olsson and Öhrman 1996) had posited that a land bridge, if not of rock, at least of ice and gravel had existed between the southern end of Gotland

and continental Europe (connecting what is now Germany) in the immediate post-glacial period. The land bridge was regarded as the means of colonisation by wild animals and possibly humans. It is now clear, however, that water has separated Gotland from the mainland from the beginning of its availability for colonisation by plants and animals. It is possible, however, that a chain of now submerged islands may have reduced the sea gaps to Gotland. Although the bathymetric data does indicate the line they would follow along the same route previously stated for the land bridge, the complex recent geological history of the area does not allow any clearer support for this hypothesis at present. How then did the hare win the race to beat the humans to the island?

According to Lindqvist and Possnert (1997), the adult hare weighs in at an average of 3.5–3.8 kilograms and like the red fox (*Vulpes vulpes*), which arrives in the archaeological remains about 1000 years after humans, may have colonised the island by passing over thin ice in the winter. In the winters of 1942 and 1947 ice was recorded stretching from Gotland all the way to the Swedish main-land, and this must be suspected to have occurred at numerous other times in the past. By the end of the Mesolithic, it is apparent that the hare is becoming very rare and this may be due to over-hunting by humans, but it is also possible that the red fox had success in taking leverets. Lindqvist and Possnert (1997) think it is possible that the fox, rather than crossing on ice, was a deliberate introduction by humans, presumably for fur, and cite a number of archaeological examples from elsewhere and other times for 'domesticated/captive' foxes.

In the later Mesolithic, with Gotland transformed from an island in a lake to an island in a sea, the subsistence repertoire is expanded to include the harp seal and harbour porpoise. Taking into account the complete Mesolithic for Gotland, the finding is that subsistence was based on non-terrestrial species with a dominance of seal, porpoise, fish and sea bird. The hare and fox make up only 1% of the faunal remains, which is very distinct compared with contemporary sites on the coast of mainland Sweden which show a strong dependence on red deer and wild boar. Lindqvist and Possnert (1999: 68) conclude that the early settlers of Gotland quickly became maritime adapted and that the use of watercraft 'was naturally a prerequisite for the human settlement of Gotland, as well as for successful sea mammal exploitation and fishing. . . .'

Clearly aquatic life was being exploited, as is the case in other communities in the circum-Baltic littoral. By the late Mesolithic, Marek Zvelebil (1996: 331) finds that:

> communities in the coastal regions of the Baltic can claim most of the attributes of a complex hunter-gatherer society: these include a degree of sedentism, high population density, more intensive food procurement, technological elaboration, development of exchange networks, social differentiation, and the emergence of territorial claims.

For Zvelebil this supposed complexity, which was enabled by access to, and specialised exploitation in seasonal schedules of, marine resources, allowed for a greater resistance to the adoption of agriculture when compared with the, by necessity, more mobile inland hunter-gatherers of continental Europe.

Unlike most Mediterranean and some Pacific islands, where, as we have seen, remnant populations of animals have survived from an earlier epoch, this is impossible for Gotland as it had been covered by hundreds of metres of ice until the beginning of the Holocene. Plants and animals can only have arrived at the end of the Ice Age. Plants are flexible colonisers, their seeds can be blown vast distances in the wind (spiders, too), and also their seeds may be dropped by birds who are themselves able to occupy islands within their flight range without great difficulty (Dennell 1983). Small mammals, such as rodents, along with small reptiles may drift to islands on vegetation. But, other than the hare and fox, when a suite of faunal introductions is made beginning 5900–5700 years ago, we can be sure that deliberate human selection is occurring.

PIGS ON GOTLAND

Zvelebil (1996) is of the opinion that the late Mesolithic communities of northwest Europe began to more carefully manage their resources through specialization in seal harvesting, the enhancement of habitats for nut harvesting (especially water chestnut and hazelnut) and closer control (perhaps even taming) of wild pigs/boars. As a package, Zvelebil (1996: 331–332) argues these 'complement each other, with the pig in the role of tame scavenger around base camps, and a source of protein and fat, with nuts as sources of carbohydrate and fodder for the pigs, and with seal and fish as food sources for people and pigs at times of seasonal abundance.'

Scholars have questioned this notion of what might be described as 'incipient agriculture', noting that all these resources were being exploited from the beginning of the Mesolithic, but we have seen in the previous chapter that a similar model has been proposed for late Pleistocene Melanesia (see Spriggs 1996). Gotland may hold the key to this proposal as here we know that pig was not present in the early Mesolithic and must be deliberately introduced if the Gotlanders were to participate in the full package as described by Zvelebil.

Pigs are introduced by humans to Gotland, but this event marks the beginning of the Neolithic (c. 5900–5700 years ago) as domestic cattle, sheep/goats and dogs also appear at this time along with signs of emmer wheat and naked barley, and associated with Funnel Beaker-style ceramics typical of northern continental Europe and southern Scandinavia (also known as *Trichterrandbecherkultur*, or TRB). Although we do not need to imagine all the elements being brought to Gotland at exactly the same time, this fairly rapid adoption of agriculture once the resistance is replaced by a willingness to experiment with new subsistence practices, is typical of coastal communities in the western Baltic, but on the eastern side a much slower rate of adoption is preferred (Zvelebil and Lillie 2000). This appears to indicate that the closer western mainland was crucial to domestic imports for Gotland. Inger Österholm (2002) finds that there is a hiatus in the use of coastal sites at this time and Early Neolithic sites are found inland in association with freshwater lakes and watercourses, a pattern typical of the Early Neolithic elsewhere in Scandinavia (Price 2000). Inger Österholm also finds that palaeoenvironmental evidence indicates a significant increase in clearing the forests by fire. So, at first glance, there is no support here for the Mesolithic package proposed by Zvelebil. However, in the Middle Neolithic (beginning c. 5200 years ago) and in association with Pitted Ware pottery, cattle and sheep/goats appear to have a significantly reduced role in the subsistence economy, which is at this time dominated by wild/feral pig and seal with cod and herring fishing (Lindqvist and Possnert 1997). It is as though, having tried farming, Gotlanders decide belatedly to take up a system of subsistence which would have been recognised on the mainland several millennia earlier, and this pattern is also repeated contemporaneously in coastal middle Sweden (Price 2000). Zvelebil (1996: 340) suggests 'that the existence of trading networks may have upheld the viability of an essentially foraging economy and delayed full adoption of farming.' It may be that the continued existence of these networks also facilitated a return to hunter-fishing subsistence.

In southern Scandinavia, the Funnel Beaker pottery is associated with the introduction of earthen long barrows for funerary purposes. No long barrows are currently known in Gotland, perhaps indicating a filtering effect in relation to what is being adopted by the indigenous people of Gotland, but in the late Early Neolithic, megalithic tombs become common in much of southern Scandinavia. An example is known from Gotland, at Gnisvärd (Ansarve) in Tofta, where the remains of at least thirty individuals have been recovered (Wallin and Martinsson-Wallin 1997). Megalithic tombs are not present on the east side of middle Sweden, and the example from Gotland may indicate the northern and eastern limit of this type of Early Neolithic monument.

The introductions to Gotland we have observed so far can be likened to the transported landscape we have witnessed for the colonisation of islands by agriculturalists in the Pacific. As we would expect, a filter effect may also be identified in that the whole package does not arrive at a single time. Explained in another way for southern Scandinavia, Zvelebil (1986) has expressed this as phases of availability, substitution and consolidation to account for the long-term process of acquiring or ignoring the items typical of the Neolithic further south in Europe. On Gotland, along with pigs, which of course in their wild variety were long exploited on the mainland, cattle, sheep/goats, dogs, grains and pottery all make an archaeologically simultaneous introduction as an apparently single Neolithic package with no obvious filtering. Dogs, which are common on Mesolithic sites in Scandinavia, may be a late introduction to Gotland due to the lack of large wild game to be hunted. An abundance of stone axe finds, palaeoenvironmental evidence for increased burning and new sites at inland locations indicate that clearing of the forests to improve pasture and provide plots for cultivation was typical of the Early Neolithic on Gotland (I. Österholm 2002).

PITTED WARE PERIOD

As commented upon above, a return to earlier maritime ways was just around the corner, and in the Middle Neolithic people abandoned their inland farms and once again inhabited coastal locations and exploited the resources of the sea. As I. Österholm (2002: 225), the excavator of a number of these sites, which are always associated with Pitted Ware pottery, has stated evocatively:

> The amount of fish and seal bones is sometimes quite incredible. It is quite apparent that the coast at the time had been in a position to offer such optimal conditions that it was possible to live very comfortably with very little effort, compared to those involved in the strenuous farm life.

Marine life may have been particularly plentiful at this time due to continuing uplift across the region as a whole, which led to significant transgressions of saline-rich water spilling in from the Atlantic. Of course, the geography of Gotland continued to change, probably being divided into a large main island with smaller islands at the north and south, all of which are parts of the main island today. Fårö had not emerged by this time. The best-known site of this period, Ajvide in Eksta Parish, is now a kilometre from the sea shore, but excavations have revealed that settlement activities spilled onto the beach in the Middle Neolithic (Burenhult 2002).

The Pitted Ware settlements are large coastal sites and were settled all year round, with associated burial grounds, and including areas for the collection of seal oil, some of which was likely exported. The overseas networks of contacts across the Baltic were not neglected as is indicated by imports in this period such as the local flint being augmented by flint from Scania (southern Sweden) and slate from Norrland (northern Sweden). However, perhaps the oddest and hardest to explain import at this time was a rather diminutive species, the hedgehog.

Hedgehogs are found on Gotland from the middle Neolithic on, and in association with Pitted Ware sites (c. 5200 to 4300 years ago), there is no doubt that they must have been deliberately imported. It is clear from the context of the recovery of their remains that they held a special importance to the people at this time. Having rejected the brief flirtation with burial in megalithic tombs, evidence from Ajvide shows that flat inhumations in the ground became the preferred method for formal disposal of the dead. At Ajvide, four of the seventy graves contained the deliberate deposition of hedgehog parts. One inhumation of a twenty-year-old female, Ajvide 2, has been nicknamed the 'Hedgehog Girl' apparently due to the presence of five hedgehog jawbones placed in a little bag on a string around her neck resting on her chest, and wearing a cap incorporating hedgehog spines (Burenhult 2002; Lindqvist and Possnert 1997). It is likely that the jaws were worn as some kind of amulet.

Burenhult has suggested that the hedgehog was some kind of animal totem for the people of Middle Neolithic Gotland. They may also have had some special significance in the Early Bronze Age of Cyclades islands in the Mediterranean, where ceramic vessels are shaped and painted to depict them (Broodbank 2000). Although this indicates that they were good to think with, they may also have been good to dine with as, although not common, hedgehogs have been recorded as a traditional food in Europe. They were particularly selected in late autumn when they had built up their reserves of fat ready for hibernation over the winter. Cooking usually requires covering the animal in clay prior to baking in an earth oven and once cooked the clay is removed, taking the spines with it and leaving the flesh on the bones for consumption (Clébert 1964). Among traveller communities, Judith Okely (1983) finds that hedgehogs enjoyed a high status and eating the liver in particular can provide medicinal and magical properties.

The graves at Ajvide were occupied by juveniles, adults, males and females, except for eight graves which were prepared and included grave goods where no burial was interred. Interestingly, Burenhult (2002) proposes that these may be cenotaphs for individuals lost at sea during fishing or seal hunting. Conversely, evidence from a Pitted Ware period grave of a young man excavated at Visby on Gotland appeared to indicate he was buried in a dugout water craft at least 3 metres in length, with harpoon, sinker and imported greenstone axe all indicating previous maritime activities (Skaarup 1995).

Besides the hedgehog remains at Ajvide, there is a rich selection of other grave goods. These include pottery, adzes/axes, fish hooks, harpoons, bone needles and amber beads. Animal remains found in the graves include boar tusks, pig, seal and brown bear. The presence of bear in the graves is interesting as there is no indication of its presence before this time or elsewhere on the island, so along with the hedgehog it may have been a deliberate introduction of the Pitted Ware users and may have also been a totem. It is interesting to note that there is no definite indication of wolf, the other large predator with the bear, being introduced at this time (Lindqvist and Possnert 1997). Clearly, selection could be due to a number of considerations, as bear too is good to eat on occasion and the pelt is very thick and useful for bedding or clothing. Of the other animals in the graves, seals and pigs are the most common throughout the domestic areas of the site, but the boar tusks are particularly favoured. Burenhult (1986) has drawn parallels with the competitive tusk growing in ethnographic examples from some Melanesian communities. In these cases, the tusks are usually transformed into personal adornments. The tusks may come from boars that have formed a feral population from the pigs introduced at the beginning of the Neolithic, although we need not assume these were domesticated in the first place (cf. Rowley-Conwy and Storå 1997). In a review of the Neolithic of eastern Sweden, Niclas Björk (2003) proposes that the communities there, which did not adopt megalithic tomb architecture, maintained an animistic/shamanistic cosmology with a closer relationship to creatures through the stronger maintenance of hunter-fisher practices. This would be a perspective developed with a view to influences more from the northeast, for example, Finland, rather than the southwest and southern Scandinavia. Perhaps this is an indication that the people of Ajvide, during the Pitted Ware period, were open to influences from the north while also maintaining contacts with the south. Once again we may be witnessing here the opportunities realised by the island community to pick and choose which external influences they preferred. Björk concludes that finds which may be linked to animistic practices and megalithic tombs are never found together, and we have already seen how the evidence for the latter is extremely limited on Gotland.

In the Late Neolithic and through to the Early Bronze Age, the people of Gotland once again turned to domesticated animals, and presumably grains, for subsistence purposes. In particular a new emphasis was placed on sheep followed by cattle, with pigs now reduced, from their previous key role, to a small component of the diet (Lindqvist and Possnert 1997). In essence, the Gotlanders fit a pattern of subsistence typical of northwest Europe at this time, indicating that influences were still being felt across the sea from the south.

■ BRONZE AGE GOTLAND

The evidence for the Bronze Age is prolific in Gotland. Round cairns, ring cairns, stone settings and field systems are extant across the island landscape. Numerous finds of bronze artefacts have been found from burials and as chance finds by metal detectorists, farmers and others. There is no source of copper on Gotland so all of these attest to importation of either raw materials or finished items. As it was in regard to the adoption of domestic animals and plants, so it was with the features and artefacts of the Bronze Age in that these were available in northwestern Europe for centuries prior to adoption in Scandinavia, beginning in Gotland about 3800 years ago.

The stone cairns which mark the Gotland landscape are typical of those found elsewhere in northwest Europe and on excavation have been found to cover burials; occasionally these are in cists. At Kauparve in Lärbo, a large cist contained an inhumation accompanied with a bronze spiral pin, and at a later stage another cist with inhumation was added with a bronze brooch as grave good. The large cairns appear to have their origins in the Early Bronze Age and can be very big indeed. One of the largest which is located at Majsterrojr in Gothem stands 4 metres high and is 33 metres in diameter, and its height is further enhanced by placement on a small hill, adding another 4 metres compared with the surrounding terrain. The cairn known as Uggarde rojr at Vinarve in Rone is 45 metres in diameter and 8 metres in height, and it is estimated that it would have stood directly adjacent to the Bronze Age shore line (Jonsonn and Lindquist 1997).

Chris Ballard and colleagues (2003), while alluding to the work of others, have suggested that in Scandinavia these large cairns, which are often located on small off-shore islands or in sight of the sea, acted as day marks to aid maritime navigation. At Kauparve, the cairn which prior to excavation was 2.7 metres high and 23 metres in diameter is situated on a cliff top that in the Bronze Age may have been the north side of a channel between two islands; and such a location perhaps indicates support for this model. Also adjacent to this area, at Hägvide, is the only significant panel of Bronze Age rock-art on Gotland. It contains dozens of cup marks, four pairs of feet, four hafted axes, and includes twenty ship motifs and these too are usually regarded as being placed in association with water. Kristian

Kristiansen (1998) suspects the routes were used to take the valued bronze artefacts north in return for furs from the high northern climes. However, many of Gotland's large cairns do not have an obvious vista to or from the sea in the present day and one suspects that Gotland itself, and the distinctive geography it would present to the seafarer at that time, would be enough of a day mark and navigational aid without requiring further enhancement from cairn building.

Ballard and colleagues (2003) comment that it may be the crossing of water as a spiritual passage that is more important than large cairns acting as beacons. This is part of a broader discussion which links depictions of sea craft in Bronze Age rock-art and inscribed on bronze artefacts, particularly razors of which there are some rare examples on Gotland, with the symbolism of water craft as a metaphor for travel over water in a society 'whose daily lives may have involved travel by sea' (2003: 398). For Kristiansen (1998), the presence of bronze artefacts in Scandinavia can only be explained by having something to trade in return. Influences from the south are also indicated in the rock-art of this period, which shows numerous illustrations of two-wheeled chariots or carts, and it might be no coincidence that horses, which are still a feature of Gotland today, may have been introduced at this time (Lindqvist and Possnert 1997). In return for such things, Kristiansen (1998) opines that beyond the furs, this might also include seal skin and oil. In this model, Gotland may either be seen as acting as an intermediary between the hunters of the north and the possessors of metals in the south, or supplying the seal products from its own resources. A combination of the two cannot be ruled out either. The intermediary role is one that holds a great deal of attractiveness because, as we shall see, it is a role that characterises the later history of the island.

SHIP-SETTINGS

The Late Bronze Age ship-settings of Gotland are a remarkable and, almost, unique feature of the island. Although some 2000 such settings are known from the circum-Baltic region, the majority of these date to the Late Iron Age or Viking Periods (Capelle 1995). Of those dating to the Bronze Age, the majority are found on Gotland, with a small cluster in western Sweden and two in Denmark. These and a couple from western Sweden date to the Early Bronze Age and are earlier than those on Gotland. One other ship-setting is found on the east coast of Sweden and two are known in Latvia. Ship-settings clearly prefigure the later examples and, indeed, actual ship burials of the Viking Period.

On Gotland the ship-settings are arranged using natural erratics or local limestone orthostats. These arrangements can be found individually, in groups, end to end, large, up to 47 metres long and 7 metres wide, such as at Gnisvärd in Tofta, or very small, although never less than 2 metres, such as the miniature ship-setting at Rannarve in Klinte (Figure 14), which is adjacent to four larger ones set end to end with stem posts 2 metres high. On occasion, the setting is filled with stones in a cairn-like structure.

In the present day, many are found in the midst of forest, but there appears to be no expectation that the sea should be in view. The setting at Gannarve in Fröjel, although much reconstructed in the twentieth century, is undoubtedly enhanced from a present-day aesthetic and interpretational perspective with its views in clear weather of the sea and the off-shore island of Lilla Karlsö (Figure front cover). Standing in the centre of one of the large settings, one immediately gets the sense of walking the deck of a ship with its full draught submerged in the water (ground) and memories of the fine lines of the clinker-built Viking ships are evoked. It is difficult to contemplate any other interpretation than that they were built to represent idealised sea craft, if not actual boats of the period, as Sven Österholm (2002: 335) proposes:

> [t]hat with their high stems and sterns and curved rails, as well as their wide shape, these stone ships are difficult to explain if one does not presume prototypes of similar design in the fleets at that time.

14. Rannarve ship-setting, Klint, Gotland (source author, 2004)

Torsten Capelle (1995: 75), who has reviewed all types of ship-settings in the region, agrees, although he believes the largest Bronze Age examples are exaggerated, and that the lack of a mast step, compared with later Viking Period examples, indicates that the contemporary craft being represented are modest rowing boats suitable for calm Baltic waters. He says what they do indicate is the presence of 'different outline forms, decks and ribs, varying side constructions, outwards sloped sides, high bow and stern [and] lengthened runner-bows. . . .'

However, as much as these were ships for the living, these are ships of the dead and typically on excavation a cremation burial is found within the bounds framed by the orthostats. For the larger settings there appears to be an inordinate amount of space defined for a single cremation; however, the effort involved in creating even the largest of these stone settings must be small in comparison to the raising of the very large cairns earlier in the Bronze Age. The cremation may not be of an individual; for example, at Rannarve the cremation deposited in a house-urn, shaped like a round house, appears to come from a funeral pyre involving a number of individuals (however, there are four ships here end to end).

At Gnisvärd (Ansarve) in Tofta, remembrances of much earlier funerary practices are perhaps being invoked by the juxtaposition of the ship-settings and the megalithic tomb. It appears clear that the ship-settings represent a manifestation of a long-standing prehistoric tradition in the Baltic region of utilising a network of seaways and symbolizing that relationship with the sea and the valued craft which allowed access to it. It is useful in the case of Gotland to go briefly beyond the normal parameters of the case studies to consider some evidence for more recent times, in order to illustrate how this endures.

IRON AGE GOTLAND

Compared with much of the rest of Europe, where inclusion in the Roman Empire brought it to an abrupt end, the Iron Age in Scandinavia is long, beginning about 2500 years ago and ending about 1200 years ago in the period when Vikings were being recorded in contemporary written documents. On occasion, the Iron Age is further divided to include the Roman Iron Age, when some influence can be detected in the form of goods from the Empire in the south, and the Migration and Vendel Periods, between the Romans and the Vikings. Of this period I wish to comment only on the peculiarly Gotlandic phenomenon of the picture stones.

The picture stones are engraved and painted dressed slabs which appear to have stood at the side of tracks and paths and through a standardised stylised form act as memorials or tombstones for deceased people. On excavation some certainly appear to mark graves. For example, at Ånge in Buttle next to Gotland's tallest picture stone standing 3.7 metres high, was uncovered a stone-lined cist grave and this too had been decorated. They are chronologically defined by shape, the earlier a flat axe shape, beginning AD 400 with blade pointing up and the second later phase ending c. AD 1100, having a mushroom-like (or keyhole) shape (further chronological distinctions have been made). Some of the later ones also include runic script, and it is in deciphering these that their memorial rather than tombstone status can be identified.

These stones have long excited scholars of the Viking era as they are assumed to depict items of clothing, weaponry and particularly water craft which illustrate sails and rigging not found in ship burials, all of which can be assumed to be proto or contemporary with the Viking Period (Burström 1996). However, the distribution of the picture stones is with only a very few exceptions exclusively Gotlandic, with approximately 440 known from the island, and must indicate something of the significance of Gotland as much or if not more than the significance of the Viking achievement. My interest is in part related to the depiction of water craft, but more so a concern as to why they are present almost exclusively on the island. I will first look briefly at the depiction of the ships and then consider the broader ramifications of the stones themselves.

Sven Österholm (2002: 335) finds that:

[t]he older picture stones on Gotland, representing the 5th century and migration period, display depictions of ships

in some cases. However, these are strongly conventionalized rowing ships, which together with some formal elements in the borders of the stones probably should be regarded as strangers, far too elegant in a Nordic Iron Age context. The canopy-like structure on the boats strengthens the impression that they have more to do with Greek vase paintings than Gotlandic Iron Age life.

Although Österholm does not think the boat represents local reality for the earliest picture stones, he appears happy in the above statement to believe it reflects a contemporary reality observed elsewhere. Certainly long-distance connections are continued through the Iron Age, as confirmed by many imports, including the Hablingo hoard of wine drinking accoutrements. However, interpretations of the picture stones have been polarised into those wishing to believe that the images reflect the contemporary reality and others who take them as providing pictorial representations of myths (cf. Burström 1996). For example, Detlev Ellmers (1995) has shown that the various repeated motifs on the picture stones can be related to specific myths clearly current during the period of manufacture. They all relate to the process of transition from life to death. The later, more complex stones illustrate the transfer of the deceased to the world of the dead and their welcome in Valhalla. According to Ellmers (1995: 170), the only peculiar thing in regard to this interpretation is the repeated presence of water craft as motifs on these stones, as mention of boats is not a feature of the myths. She suggests as a possibility that

> people in continental Scandinavia did not think boats to be necessary for the voyage to Valhalla. But surely in Gotland everybody would be convinced that the voyage to Valhalla could not be done without a ship.

Thus, Gotland's maritime connections are being appealed to in order to make the myths make sense in the local context. The later picture stones show sailing ships with large square sails, complex net-like rigging and carrying armed men, who are often holding round shields. The shape of the hull coincides with that found from ship burials and presumably indicates that although a myth may be being represented, the individual elements can be relied upon to provide an insight into actual ship design and use at that time. Clearly, as Ellmers (1995) points out, you will not be expecting to be carried to the realm of the dead on a cargo vessel, so not all types of vessels are likely depicted.

How can we interpret these stones in relation to the islanders' perception and place in the world at this time? Given that they are rare elsewhere, should we assume that this links insularity with isolation? Clearly, this would be ridiculous, for not only do the stones speak of overseas contacts in pictures and runes, reflecting technological and linguistic changes over time and identified elsewhere, but also the contemporary archaeology is rich in imported items with hundreds of silver hoards indicating contacts either direct or down the line linking with the Atlantic and the Mediterranean. Late Saxon coins from England, including an exceptionally large amount from the mint in Lydford in Devon, and coins from the Arabic world all indicate that from the eighth to eleventh centuries Gotland is involved in a wider world.

Dan Carlsson (e.g., 1991) has located abundant evidence of ports both small and large operating as harbours for trading vessels at this time. He sees this proliferation coming into being following a long development 'going right back to prehistoric times' (1991: 147). It is clear from the review above that he must be right. Is there something distinctive about the Baltic Sea which would favour such long-term developments leading to an explosion of long-distance voyaging in the Viking Age?

THE BALTIC SEA

Properly speaking, the Baltic Sea is a gulf of the Atlantic Ocean, although for all intents and purposes it is an inland sea with a passage to the North Sea. At 373,000 square kilometres, including the Bothnian Sea and Gulf, the Gulf of Finland and Riga Bay, it is the biggest body of brackish water in the world, acting as an outlet for rivers on all sides. The saline solution is low compared with the Atlantic Ocean, with the Baltic having a maximum of 1.5%, although often much less, compared with 3.5% in the Atlantic. This, of course, limits the species of flora and fauna able to survive in this environment. The Baltic is also a shallow body of water with an average depth of only 60 metres.

As stated above, the distances to mainland or other islands from Gotland are relatively small. The land encloses the sea and may provide the type of maritime nursery discussed in previous chapters. There is also very little in the way of a tidal range and in the summer a southwesterly wind can usually be relied upon. In the winter, ice can be a problem. Seafaring was, for the most part, restricted to the summer months. Sven Österholm (2002) has studied in detail the possibilities of prehistoric seafaring in the Baltic and constructed two experimental vessels. The first, a dugout of lime tree some 4 metres long with an outrigger, was successfully paddled by two crew the 4 nautical miles from Gotland's shore to Stora Karlsö, averaging a speed of 2 knots. The second, *Alkraku II*, was rather more ambitious and hewn from a poplar log 7.5 metres long with a maximum diameter of 75 centimetres. This had a 4.7-metre outrigger of spruce, four outrigger beams of hazel and a mast 4.7 metres tall of spruce. The dugout was deepened by the addition of bound double boards in clinker (overlapping) style. This was successfully paddled and sailed by five crew from Gotland to Öland and then on to the mainland (at a later date it was taken to Scania, Denmark and Germany). The findings of this voyage suggested the crossing to Öland could have been paddled in 8–9 hours or sailed in a fair wind in 6–7 hours. On a clear day, such a crossing would have taken a period of approximately an hour where land could not be seen in any direction. However, Österholm found that navigation would not be a problem as the 'eternal' southwesterly swell of the Baltic could be keenly felt through the craft, an experience not unfamiliar to that observed in traditional Pacific navigation as discussed in Chapter 2.

As is typical of such experiments, one can complain that modern materials were used and the design was not one based on actual archaeological examples. The choice of wood rather than skin was made on the basis that this option would only be used where decent wood was in short supply. Clinker construction techniques were applied in the belief that as a development of the dugout canoe, this was the second most 'ancient' type of construction in Scandinavia. Österholm did test some materials which would have been available to boat builders in prehistory, and although he would have preferred seal skin for the sail material he had to settle for flax. His design was based on Melanesian ethnography, some experience of building traditional Gotlandic craft and the depictions of boats from the rich corpus of Scandinavian rock-art usually attributed to Bronze Age carvers (this latter is, however, rather rare on Gotland).

According to Österholm, the attachment of an outrigger caused particular consternation to observers as there is no tradition of its use in northwest Europe. It is the rock-art which provides the clue to the use of such technology in prehistory. Österholm argues convincingly, I think, that the motifs usually interpreted as boats should be understood as 'gatefold illustrations' in which parts of the feature are folded out so that their presence can be illustrated, but where in a normal perspective these would be hidden or hard to represent. For example, in this model a four-wheeled cart may be illustrated as a rectangle with two wheels on either side apparently lying flat and joined to the rectangle by a short line. Such depictions can be found in European prehistoric rock-art, and such a perspective was common in art until the Renaissance. With this model in mind, the illustrations of the types of boats in Scandinavian rock-art have occasionally been interpreted as sleighs. The bottom line is not illustrating a rather odd-looking hull of the craft or the skate of a sled, but the outrigger of the craft. Some examples have crosses which may illustrate the beam attachments, and others have depictions of what might be sails. The depictions of water craft become conventionalised over time, losing the detailed attachments to the original.

Österholm (2002: 327) further supports his argument that sails would have been available in some form or other by the observation made when in the first experimental craft that standing up in a fresh breeze caught the wind and provided momentum to the boat, an 'effect [that] cannot have escaped prehistoric seafarers.' Also, he comments on a direct observation he made in the mid-twentieth century in Finland where a 5-kilometre lake passage was completed using an unmodified leafy birch tree as a sail! His argument is that the advantages are obvious and the means easily available.

CONCLUSION

It is likely that the geography of the Baltic Sea basin provided, from the Mesolithic onwards, the type of conditions which favoured the development of maritime technology and skills. That the inhabitants of Gotland were intimately linked to these developments was likely. I am not here supporting what Burström (1996: 33) has called 'chauvinistic' interpretations of Gotlandic history; '[a]ccording to this, Gotland has been the cultural centre in the Baltic region for several thousand years.' Rather, the archaeology of Gotland indicates parallel developments with areas of the circum-Baltic littoral in all periods of its history. The island's position at the centre of the Baltic Sea has allowed influences to be received from all directions, but these have not always been taken up. The nature of the Baltic coast, with its fjords and offshore islands, means that elsewhere in the region water craft have also been essential for daily life since the land was freed of its capping of ice. Gotland was so located to take advantage of this situation and often did to great profit. This also did not preclude the development and presentation of a distinct identity to many visitors from elsewhere, as Burström (1996: 32) has stated cogently:

The Gotlandic identity is very strong indeed. Both the islanders themselves and outsiders think there exists something genuinely Gotlandic that separates the island and its inhabitants from the rest of Sweden. . . . A central part of the Gotlandic identity is . . . Gotland's history.

Do we here have another example of continuous and expected contacts with others breeding specific traits of social identity? In mediaeval times, and today part of the proud Gotlandic heritage, the islanders built a stupendous number of churches (perhaps read temples or *moai*). This huge investment of labour and wealth was not due to some crises of isolation, an impending environmental catastrophe or inbreeding, or even a final profligate plea to God as a saviour, but the result of huge wealth on the island generated by Visby and Gotland's membership of the Hanseatic League, a group of trading partners who monopolized the seaways of the north at that time.

7

Atlantic Archipelago

The Western Seaways of Europe

The Atlantic Archipelago, formed by Britain and Ireland (Figure 15), may seem an odd choice for a case study in a book about the archaeology of islands as they are rarely discussed within the terminology and constructions of island archaeology. Archaeologists in Britain and Ireland rarely conceive of their work as taking place in an island setting, and the modern political boundaries have reduced conceptions of parameters based in the locations of land and sea. As a native of these islands, I too am of this opinion. The large islands of Britain and Ireland are conceptually, if not biogeographically, mainlands. There is a relativity at play here. Mike Parker Pearson (2004) has noted that his work on Madagascar, an island well over twice the size of Britain, is easily conceptualised by colleagues as island archaeology, but few consider their British work to be island-based.

15. Map of the Atlantic Archipelago (drafted by H. Wilson)

Another example is Tasmania, the 'Apple Isle', off the southeast coast of the island-continent of Australia. It is about two-thirds the size of Ireland in area and is conceptualised by inhabitants and outsiders as an island. Tasmania, of course, has a significant role in the conceptualisation of islands in archaeology due to the identification that the inhabitants met by early European explorers had originally arrived on the island by walking to the then peninsula during the last Ice Age when lower sea levels left the land, later to be submerged under Bass Strait, dry and traversable. As sea levels rose at the end of the Pleistocene, the Tasmanians were apparently left stranded. For Rhys Jones (1977) this explained the impoverished suite of material culture and subsistence base when compared with mainland indigenous groups and led to his now famous phrase that in their isolation the Tasmanians suffered 'a slow strangulation of the mind' (1977: 202). Although large, it is easy to conceptualise Tasmania (60,640 km^2) as an island because of its position in relation to the much larger Australian mainland.

Ireland is smaller than Britain, but is adjacent to Britain, visible on clear days, and even on miserable days, for example, from the Mull of Kintyre. Britain is adjacent to its continent, with only 34 kilometres (21 miles) separating the two coasts at their narrowest point. Such proximity breeds a notion of a peninsula rather than an island, part of Europe, but slightly different; the sea provides clearer but still fuzzy boundaries. And it is the sea in a sense on which I intend to focus in this chapter. It is here, using the archaeology of the Atlantic Archipelago, that I wish to highlight further the benefits of conceptualising a maritime-focussed prehistory, in considering a connected sea, particularly that of the western seaways, which I will show is essential for understanding much of the archipelago's prehistory from the Neolithic through to the Iron Age. We will see, especially by using the evidence of the many smaller islands which constitute significant elements of the archipelago from Shetland in the north to Scilly in the southwest, that the sea as a means of communication has connected the island communities with the European continent for as long as it has been there to do so since the end of the Pleistocene. We will also see how the sailing nurseries of the Aegean and Baltic eventually converged in the Atlantic Archipelago.

▪ WESTERN SEAWAYS

Since the first half of the twentieth century, geographers and archaeologists recognised the influence of the sea for understanding of the human history of the Atlantic Archipelago. Much of the focus was on maritime routes connecting large parts of the central Archipelago, that is, on the east side of Ireland and west side of Britain. Routes were envisaged plying in both directions through and across the Irish and Celtic Seas (i.e., the north and south basins of the Irish Sea, respectively) and heading south to the Bristol Channel (Severn Sea), the southwest peninsula of Britain and to Brittany, France and Galicia, Spain and beyond and in the north passing through the Minches (North Channel) between the Inner and Outer Hebrides and continuing to the Northern Isles of Orkney and Shetland and beyond, towards the Faeroes, Iceland and Scandinavia. Jonathan Wooding (1996) has reviewed the character of the western seaways, noting the coastal geography, prevailing winds, currents, tides and shoals and offshore rocks. Although sympathising with the Mediterranean perspective found in Julius Caesar's view that 'the Atlantic was as fearsome an opponent as the Veneti themselves' whom he was trying to defeat, Wooding concludes:

> The societies which have existed along the western sealanes have regularly navigated these forbidding waters, finding various technological solutions to the conditions. Initially disconcerting, the conditions command respect, but are not so terrifying as to compel travellers to go overland by preference, or to support arguments regarding the unsuitability of certain types of craft – such as currachs – for long-distance voyaging. At all times, however, the geographical factors render some choices of route and ship design more effective than others. (Wooding 1996: 6)

Thus, it is the long-term experience of these waters which is essential and, as such, it is not surprising that a number of the scholars of the western seaways were based at the University in Aberystwyth, where it is easy to imagine that the vista from their windows overlooking Cardigan Bay and the Irish Sea beyond helped shape their perspectives. One of these, Emrys G. Bowen, was Professor of Geography and Anthropology, and can perhaps be regarded as the last great advocate of the western seaways concept in its first phase. Bowen (1970, 1972) provides a history of the development of thinking on this matter. Beginning with geographer H. J. Mackinder's 1902 statement that from the end of the Ice Age, Ireland had become 'insulated' and 'divided' from Britain and Europe, he finds that the weight of evidence from archaeology was not yet there to doubt this conclusion, but also interestingly, that scholars of the period who had been educated in classical traditions were influenced by concepts of the Roman Empire where 'the sea divides; the land unites' and, of course, Ireland remained independent from Roman imperialism. Bowen finds this view is changed through the works of O. G. S. Crawford, H. J. Fleure and Sir Cyril Fox. Bowen remarks that the influence of such work allowed Gordon Childe to speak of the Irish Sea quite differently from that imagined by Mackinder in having 'grey waters as bright with Neolithic argonauts as the western Pacific is today' (quoted in Bowen 1970: 14). This view of the western seaways was taken up with vigour and the western seaways became identified as the source for everything from megalithic tombs (Daniel 1941) to Celtic Christianity (Bowen 1969; see Wooding 1996 for a detailed review). However, although such other luminaries as Christopher Hawkes, Stuart Piggott, Ralegh Radford and Charles Thomas had found good uses for the concept, in the 1970s few other academic scholars shared such vistas and, with prehistorians rejecting migrationist and diffusionist views of culture history, the western seaways fell out of favour.

However, in the twenty-first century, the western seaways are back, not that they completely went away, as illustrated in the review by Cummings and Fowler (2004). Many scholars are now finding the role of communication by sea a useful explanatory framework for understanding both similarities and differences in the material remains in various periods of the prehistoric past (e.g., Cunliffe 2001). The nuanced interpretations available derived from the debates following the rejection of culture history as a descriptive and explanatory device means that archaeologists are now better able to interrogate and interpret exotic material and proxy indicators as evidence of overseas, and perhaps regular, contact, without compromising understandings of local identity and difference. As we shall see, this has opened a new chapter for the western seaways and maritime prehistory in the Atlantic Archipelago.

MESOLITHIC PRELUDE?

Britain was connected to the continent by dry land during the Mesolithic period. Eventually as the glaciers retreated, low-lying areas, now submerged by the Bristol Channel and the North Sea, became flooded and finally the English Channel/*La Manche* formed and Britain became separated from the continent by a stretch of sea. Like the colonisers of Tasmania, the ancestors of the inhabitants of the new island had originally walked there. During the Mesolithic, it is generally considered that the inhabitants of the North Sea plain shared many cultural similarities with the groups inhabiting southern Scandinavia, so much so that they are given a shared name, the Maglemosian. However, although as we have seen in the previous chapter the southern Scandinavian Mesolithic is characterised by its use and relationship with maritime resources, the evidence for Britain is much less compelling, and this absence has generally been regarded as resulting from sea level rise destroying the archaeological remains of this period. A number of shell middens and related sites have been found in Scotland where the removal of the ice allowed the land to rebound and rise in relation to sea level. Such sites include a number of islands in the Inner Hebrides, including the islands of Rum, Oronsay, Islay and possible indications of a presence in the

Orkneys and Outer Hebrides; they would, of course, have required boats to access and utilise these places.

A further indication that maritime skills must have been present in the Mesolithic population is provided by the probable deliberate seaborne colonization of Ireland across what was likely a narrower Irish Sea than the present day. Ireland in the immediate post-glacial period holds some similarities with Gotland in that the retreating ice and fast onset of insularity allowed the opportunity for only a reduced population of wild animal species to establish itself ahead of humans. Peter Woodman (2000) sees the lack of large mammals reflected in the Mesolithic stone tool kit, which is macrolithic, and evidently non-piercing (i.e., not for projectile purposes), when compared to the microlith technology of Britain. Based on a critical analysis of dates and contexts of recovery, Woodman and McCarthy (2003; also Tresset 2003) propose that domestic cattle may have been introduced in Ireland during what traditionally would be called the Late Mesolithic. There is no evidence for wild cattle prior to this. They continue that these may have served to supplement the faunal subsistence base. Approximately 6200 years ago, the source of the cattle would have to be continental Europe, possibly southern Brittany or the Loire coastal region. They further speculate that wild boar may have been another sea-borne introduction in the Mesolithic. The mixture of wild and domestic in the assemblages of Late Mesolithic Ireland both indicates a distinction with other parts of the archipelago and illustrates that the availability frontier as discussed in the previous chapter can be one where a connecting sea can allow connections in previously unexpected directions.

ARRIVALS (AND DEPARTURES?)

The Neolithic in the Atlantic Archipelago is a highly contested space, with the chronology, particularly the date of the beginning of the period, constantly being questioned. The evidence of non-indigenous domesticated animals is supposed to mean migration of people with these from the continent or alternatively the adoption of them by indigenous communities. But the role of these domesticates is also questioned as to whether they are representative of sedentary farmers or mobile populations following similar cycles of movement across the landscape to their Mesolithic forebears. This scenario envisages having some herding and planting as only a minor addition to the pre-Neolithic subsistence base, along with adopting some other practices, such as pottery making and tomb building, typical of the Neolithic on the continent. It is not my intention to enter into these debates here, although my discussion will touch on some of the key issues and certainly uses evidence that is often vital to the polarised arguments. My main concern is in identifying mobility in the western seaways. This is different from the mobility of gatherer-hunter-fisher populations mentioned above in that this is not about cycles of movement within a territory, but rather longer distance communication using the sea as a pathway.

That long-distance seaborne interaction did occur at the beginning of the Neolithic in the Atlantic Archipelago cannot be doubted; the presence of sheep and goats in the material remains of this time provides proxy evidence for this. As we have seen in previous chapters, sheep/goats were not found as a wild variety in Europe and in every circumstance must be an introduction. In the case of islands this must be deliberate. Accepting that sheep and goats were derived from populations in western Europe, archaeologists have looked to other indicators of such contacts. For decades the architecture and construction of megalithic chambered tombs have been scrutinised in order to find indications of contacts between areas within the Atlantic Archipelago and beyond to the continent (Figure 16).

Following strongly in this tradition, Alison Sheridan (2003a) has argued that the megalithic grave site and associated artefacts excavated at Achnacreebeag in Argyll, western Scotland, are so closely related to Neolithic remains in Brittany, western France, that this is evidence of the migration of a group of people from France to Scotland, very early in the Neolithic, some 6200 to 5900 years ago.

16. Pentre Ifan, Pembrokeshire, Wales, UK. This chambered tomb is situated on a hill and allows views to Cardigan Bay and the Irish Sea beyond (source author, 2003)

As an extension to this finding, Sheridan finds other examples of the closed chamber and simple passage tombs (passage graves) in Wales undated and in Ireland, where she finds the evidence from Carrowmore in County Sligo, western Ireland provides compellingly similar dates (Sheridan 2003b). Whether one accepts the hypothesis or not, similar dates from sites in the Irish Sea may perhaps be indicating that a maritime-based early/earliest Neolithic is related to western seaways and removes the emphasis from southern England in relation to the earliest significant contacts and sharing of practices and materials. Anne Tresset (2003) has critically reconsidered the evidence of domestic cattle and sheep from a midden on offshore Dalkey Island in Dublin Bay and finds a date in the region of 6000 years ago likely. On the Isle of Man, centred in the north Irish Sea basin and in the main stream of the western seaways, Timothy Darvill (2001) in excavations and surveys has established that structures and materials typical of the Neolithic elsewhere in the Atlantic Archipelago were also present here by 6000 years ago. Although there are the inherent vagaries of dating, it is possible that contacts with Neolithic communities in western France, utilising the western seaways, led to the introduction of recognisably Neolithic animals, domesticated sheep and cattle and novel ways of dealing with the dead up to two centuries before they are witnessed in southern England, which is geographically speaking significantly closer to the continent. To this list we may add pottery, according to Sheridan (2003a), in relation to the finds at Achnacreebeag, but ceramics are less well associated with the early dates elsewhere.

At the beginning of the Neolithic, it appears that there is a strong possibility that seafaring skills and technologically competent vessels allowed contacts between western France, the Irish Sea, the west coast of Scotland and the west coast of Ireland, the latter beyond relatively sheltered waters, although similar conditions would be met from the crossing from France to St George's Channel at the entrance to the Celtic and Irish Seas. Graham Clark (1977) proposed that the distribution of megalithic tomb types on the Atlantic seaboard could be reflective of sea-fishing, particularly hake and mackerel, whose shoals frequent these areas. Parts of these seaways had already been traversed by Mesolithic peoples, and it is a moot point to ask who were the prime movers in this movement. Robin Dennell (1983) once suggested that Neolithic farmers with boats were about as useful as the Swiss having a navy, but as we have already seen farmers did use boats and often. The polarised distinctions between gatherer-hunters and farmers are not as clear as they once appeared to be. In any case, although Mesolithic people had probably been there before, the northerly limit of these seaways in the earliest Neolithic appears to be western Scotland, as Orkney and Shetland do not appear to be settled by users of Neolithic animals and materials until several centuries later, at around 5600 years ago.

When the Orkney Islands are settled, it appears to be through an extension of the western seaways which facilitates this. Artefact types, especially the Unstan Ware type pottery, and similarities in monumental tomb architecture indicate that the Outer Hebrides provided the ideas and probably the people (Parker Pearson 2004).

At the artificial island crannog of Eileen Domhnuill in Loch Olabhat on North Uist, Ian Armit (2003) has excavated an Early Neolithic settlement, producing large amounts of pottery some of which has Orcadian connections. The location of this site constructed in a freshwater lake may indicate an early cosmological interest in bodies of water, also recognised in late Neolithic Orkney by Colin Richards (1996). During the first part of the Neolithic, the Outer Hebrides and the Orkney Islands appear from the material culture to be following similar social trajectories. Parker Pearson (2004) has noted that the density of megalithic tombs and cairns on these islands (and Arran) is greater than equivalent areas of land on the neighbouring mainland.

Gabriel Cooney (2004) has opined that islands themselves may become regarded as monuments, noting in particular the distinctive 340-metre-high dome shape of Ailsa Craig which also marks the entrance to the Firth of Clyde (Figure 17). Peter Davey (2004) has speculated regarding the role of the Isle of Man in creation myths for the island and a figure, Mannanán, known in Scotland and Ireland. Suggestions that the megalithic tombs were important for maritime navigation as daymarks sighted from the sea (Phillips 2003) or linked to placing the dead in the liminal zone between sea and land provided

17. **Ailsa Craig, Firth of Clyde, Scotland, UK. Island as monument? (source author, 1988)**

by the coast (Scarre 2002, for Brittany tombs) are not convincing in these small island situations. Interestingly, Davey (2004) notes a folk tradition in the Isle of Man of fishermen using the enigmatic Neolithic stone setting at Meayll Circle (Mull Hill) as a daymark to locate a favoured fishing ground, though it is unlikely to have been one of its primary functions. Perhaps, as has been proposed for the impressive and contemporary standing stone setting of Callanish on Lewis (Cole Henley, pers. comm.), in the Outer Hebrides, we should consider the density of such monuments on these islands as indicators of movement along the pathways provided by the sea (cf. Tilley 1994).

In the Late Neolithic, the trajectories of Orkney and the Hebrides appear to diverge with the building of monumental architecture, including the potential Orcadian innovations of the henge monument and Grooved Ware ceramics finding their way south, most likely through the western seaways, but bypassing the Hebrides where the islanders appear to resist adopting these (Parker Pearson 2004). A similar situation to the Hebrides appears in the Isle of Man in this period (Burrow 1999) and although leaping ahead in time slightly it does appear that in the Bronze Age, from the very beginning of that period, both the Hebrides and Man rejoin the mainstream, illustrating the succession of pottery types expected elsewhere in the Atlantic Archipelago (Woodcock 2004). Orkney now appears to be resisting the new innovations with perhaps the islanders attempting to hold on to their past glories (Parker Pearson 2004). Interestingly, the spatial distribution for the disposal of the dead changes in the Bronze Age and is comparable to that discussed in southern Scandinavia, with burial cairns often placed on small off-shore islands (Branigan and Foster 2002), with similar implications related to the crossing of water and death discussed in the previous chapter.

In the Hebrides and the Northern Islands, a further proxy indicator of communication along the seaways is provided by importation of specific types of stone for tools. Bloodstone from Rum is found in Orkney and the intervening islands; pitchstone from Arran is found in the Hebrides, along with polished stone axes with an origin in northern Ireland. Gabriel Cooney (2004) has discussed not only this prosaic indicator of communication but the potential potency of stones from island sources which, when taken from the island, acted to link to the power of the island. Cooney notes the difficulties inherent, due to currents and tidal races, of gaining access to quarry porcellanite on Rathlin Island. Rathlin is located off the northeast tip of Northern Ireland and marks the northwestern side of the Northern Channel in to the Irish Sea. Another source of porcellanite is available on the Irish mainland and it too was exploited in the Neolithic, but Cooney proposes that the association with Rathlin would likely make that material more highly favoured. Of course, a similar argument has been made for the difficulty of access to the Langdale stone source high on a mountainside in the Lake District (Bradley and Edmonds 1993), and illustrates that islands are not unique in providing such arenas for developing powerful associations between source, extraction and artefact. But, of course, axes from the Langdale source find their way in large numbers across the Irish Sea, and the porcellanite axes from northern Ireland are found in England and Wales. There is a particular concentration of finds in northeast Scotland, perhaps indicating that the inland waterways of the Great Glen too may be linked to the western seaways at this time. A more direct northerly use of the western seaways is indicated by the large amounts of gabbro axes, up to 383 identified so far, from a source in Cornwall which are found in Ireland (Cooney and Mandal 1998; Ray 2004). Of course, travel by sea in itself may enhance the reputation of an axe.

It is likely that outside the sphere of the western seaways, separate, probably numerous cross-channel contacts were being made which led to the slightly later introduction of Neolithic elements in southern England. Tresset's (2003) faunal analyses comparing contemporary northern French and southern English remains indicate this, as does the passage grave at Broadsands near Paignton on the south Devon coast (Sheridan 2003b). This example highlights a lacuna in the evidence for the western seaways connections in the early Neolithic as there are no sites in the southwest peninsula or indeed the Isles of Scilly that, as yet, can be dated to this time. Indeed, it is generally regarded that there was no human presence on the Scillies at this time. However, the fact that much of the land from that period is now submerged, Charles Thomas's (1985) 'drowned landscape', may indicate a reason for the difficulties for finding such sites in the southwest (Mercer 2003). Of course, we should not forget that comparable sites in Brittany may also have been lost due to evident submergence that has occurred there since the Neolithic.

In a review of prehistoric island use along what they term the 'Atlantic Façade', Rick Schulting and colleagues (2004) find that although there is evidence for Mesolithic visitation, the evidence points to the majority of the islands, including relatively large ones such as the Outer Hebrides and Northern Isles, being settled for the first time in the Neolithic, with the majority settled by 5000 years ago. The point Schulting and colleagues make is that, despite their maritime location, the faunal remains and isotopic analyses of human bones indicate that these islands are settled for predominantly terrestrial reasons. They point to the relatively mild climate of the west coast due to the Gulf Stream and allowing for a longer growing season. The authors also stress the advantages of keeping your valuable domestic animals on small islands where they have a natural boundary, allowing easier control and safety from predators. Schulting and colleagues recognise that these reasons will not completely explain the attractiveness of islands for people in the Neolithic, but argue that any maritime advantage is only minimally exploited. This is indeed an interesting point, and if they are correct, it provides a timely corrective to assuming that maritime societies necessarily have to eat fish (contra Jones 1977 and the Tasmanians commented on above). In the same way as modern studies find that sailors often do not swim and do not want to learn, they do not necessarily have to eat the products of the sea. Or to put it another way, they do not consume the marine products of the sea, as arguably the sheep and cattle are products of the sea, having been imported in the first place.

Another feature of small islands, similar to their suitability for pastoralism, according to Schulting and colleagues (2004), is their use for herding wild animals. However, on Orkney they find minimal evidence for wild animals in the assemblages and indeed propose that the red deer antlers recovered from Knap of Howar on Papa Westray had been imported. More abundant evidence from sites dating to later in the Neolithic in Orkney and in Ireland where red deer are not present in the Mesolithic, and only represented by antler finds in Early Neolithic contexts, have led to suggestions that these are a deliberate introduction (Sharples 2000; Woodman and McCarthy 2003). In both cases the authors argue that this introduction may have been to more easily procure the antlers for use in special rites and objects rather than to enhance the subsistence base. Introduction for such purposes perhaps compares to the introduction of hedgehog and bear to Gotland for apparently similar non-economic reasons.

Andrew Fleming (2005), following archaeological investigations on the archipelago of St Kilda, has provided further evidence for maritime connections at this time. The evidence he presents is that the Late Neolithic settlers of these islands, located 65 kilometres west of the Outer Hebrides, did not find interaction with their closest neighbours but with the Northern Islands of Orkney and Shetland. Fleming (2005: 54) concludes that given the previous prevailing view of isolation

> prehistorians will have to think long and hard about why St. Kilda was apparently so closely linked to the Northern Isles and what this may mean for our understanding of maritime skills and long-distance contacts four or five thousand years ago.

Certainly, at the very least it suggests that the distance/size ratio and nearest neighbour analyses used by adherents to the biogeographic approaches to the study of islands can be confounded by human intentionality. Ancestry and alliances may play roles here, but the earliest links as we have seen are supposed to be between the Outer Hebrides and the Orkneys. Perhaps those links double-back beyond the Hebrides to St Kilda, which may have been already well known for its abundant seabird resources? St Kilda is visible from high points on the Outer Hebrides in clear conditions, including from Barra where heeled-cairns may indicate a link with Shetland at this time (Branigan and Foster 2002). The excavation of a likely Bronze Age stone boat-setting on St Kilda, bearing comparison with small examples from Gotland, led Tony Pollard (1999) to propose that the likely funerary nature of the monument acted as a cenotaph to those bodies which may have been lost at sea.

There can be no doubt that communication by sea continued through the Neolithic and is indicated by various stone resources and the development of monuments unique to the Archipelago, such as henge monuments found from Orkney to Wessex. It is instructive that Darvill (2004: 48) has characterised the Neolithic of the Isle of Man as a 'nested scheme of cultural interaction' involving distinctive features of local identity while sharing in common experiences and translations of that experience from a much broader area. So the presence of long barrows and a common organisation and inclusion of special stones in their façades, the deliberate curation and deposition of quartz pebbles and a focus on pit digging all can be seen as typical of a much broader region. Additionally, the specific style of pottery and the uses to which it is put indicate a distinctiveness related to an islander identity.

Arrivals and departures in the Neolithic do not always leave a physical manifestation. Neolithic elements introduced from the continent became fused and transformed through experiences in the Archipelago. Regional differences developed in ways similar to that described by Darvill, but the evidence from Wessex, Orkney and Ireland in the later Neolithic is that if there had been any waning of the contacts after the earlier Neolithic, the shared experiences of materials and monuments showed it was back with a vengeance and including links to the continent. In the Late Neolithic/beginning of the Bronze Age, metal artefacts of bronze and gold, pottery of distinctive Beaker style, and the introduction of the horse to Ireland show that the scale of seaborne communication continued unabated. We may also include on this list the rock-art, which at this time consists of geometric engravings commonly termed 'cup and ring marks'. The distribution of these engravings has as its focus western and northern Britain, although Wales and particularly the southwest peninsula of England are not well endowed with them. Richard Bradley (1997) has proposed that the engravings form a tradition of rock-art related to contacts along the Atlantic seaways from the Iberian Peninsula to northern Scotland. The Bronze Age provides the first evidence of the actual sea craft used in these journeys.

'ATTENTION ALL SHIPPING' – BRONZE AGE BOATS

The majority and most complete direct evidence for seafaring technology allowing communication within and beyond the Atlantic Archipelago does not come from the region directly influenced by the western seaways, but rather the east and southeast of Britain. Cooney (2004), in reviewing briefly the evidence for prehistoric sea craft in the Irish Sea, notes two types of vessels in the region: (1) beginning in the Mesolithic, the very long tradition of log boats which, with a little modification, may have been used for fair weather open sea travel, but for the most part used in inland waterways; and (2) the proxy evidence for hide-covered boats existing in the Neolithic as indicated by later period models from Caergwle in Flintshire, Wales (contra McGrail 1990) and from Broighter, County Derry, Ireland. Cooney envisages hide-covered keeled *currachs*, a type known historically in Ireland, plying the western seaways from the Neolithic onwards (Figure 18). Plank-built craft have been generally considered less likely in the western seaways due to a supposed lack of suitable timber on these exposed and damp coasts, but it can also equally be questioned, particularly for Ireland, as to where the large mammals were found to provide hides for *currachs* in the earliest periods. Both hides and wood can be imported (by people with the appropriate sea craft), as can complete vessels. The presence of both hide and plank traditions in the western seaways should not at this

18. Stowed *currachs*, Dingle Peninsula, Ireland (source author, 2003)

stage be excluded. Indeed, two Bronze Age find sites of plank boats are known from the Welsh side of the Severn Estuary at the head of the Bristol Channel at Caldicot and Goldcliff (Nayling and Caseldine 1997). The Caldicot find dates from the earlier Bronze Age and is thus comparable to the better preserved boats from Dover, Kent and North Ferriby on the Humber Estuary. Plank boats are regarded as more stable and robust craft than hide boats and the sewn-plank design may be an innovation based on the earlier sewing of hides (Van de Noort 2004). However, Mercer (2003) has pointed out that an advantage of hide boats is that they are lighter and more easily carried or hauled across the isthmus of a peninsula to avoid the potential dangers of rounding headlands by sea. Perhaps maritime communities chose the best type for the purpose and destination of the journey they intended (cf. Clark 2004a)?

Although they are generally accepted as representative of sea-going craft, there is some debate as to whether either the proposed plank or hide craft were really capable of the open sea passages usually claimed. The Ferriby craft only provided ferry services across the Humber (see review by Coates 2005), and doubt has been expressed in regard to the Dover boat (Marsden 2004). However, circumstantial evidence based on the presence of marine sand, the nature of the local environment in the Bronze Age and the size of the craft has led to the conclusion that the Dover boat was coastal or seagoing (Clark 2004a). Like the Ferriby vessels, the Dover boat is constructed of oak planks stitched together using yew withies and caulked with moss and honey and 14 metres long and 2.25 metres wide. Peter Clark (2004a, 2004b) has proposed that it functioned as a cargo vessel with a crew of sixteen and a 3-tonne capacity and probably plying the south coast of Britain. The flat base of the hull, although creating doubts about its seaworthiness, allows for beaching with an ebbing tide, loading the cargo and allowing the incoming tide to refloat the craft. A piece of shale from Kimmeridge in Dorset found in the vessel indicates this directionality, although Clark thinks the preferred cargo would be copper, tin and/or bronze objects from the ore-rich southwest peninsula and all in high demand in ore-poor southeast England. In the classic paradoxical statement of maritime archaeology, the finds of bronze artefacts from probable wreck sites at Salcombe in south Devon and from near Dover itself, show that such cargoes were being transported in this region in the Bronze Age. We may tentatively add to this the tin ingots recovered from the sea floor at the mouth of the estuary of the river Erme, located close to Salcombe and also on the south Devon coast (Fox 1995).

The Dover Boat is dated to approximately 3500 years ago, a time when islands in the western Pacific were being settled by sea passages of hundreds and occasionally over 1000 kilometres (see Chapter 5). This observation provides an interesting comparison in regards to the perhaps at first sight over-exuberant claims of Clark (2004b: 7) for the seafaring context of the Dover Boat. In considering the terrestrial archaeology of both sides of the channel, similarities in artefact type, house form and funerary practice suggest that:

> there was a higher level social grouping that straddled the channel, that rather than 'trade' or 'exchange' between different ent groups either side of the water they were a single 'people'

or 'tribe' bound together by close social (perhaps familial) and economic relationships; 'the people of La Manche'.

Clark (2004b) goes on to note that the journey from Dover to the nearest contemporary site in France is 55 kilometres, although the coastal voyages attested by the shale in the Dover Boat and a nearby find of a Trevisker type urn from Cornwall indicate distances travelled of 220 and 450 kilometres, respectively. So the cross-channel route, with either side easily seen on a clear day, may have allowed by the end of the earlier Bronze Age the establishment of a maritime community utilising the English Channel/ *La Manche* with connections stretching along the south coast of Britain at least as far as the southwest peninsula and the edge of the western seaways, and cross-channel to France. With materials and artefacts in bronze, amber and gold forming elements of contemporary material culture, there are indications that these connections stretched north to Scandinavia and south to the Alps. As we saw in Chapter 6 in relation to Gotland, ultimately the contacts draw together the Atlantic and the Mediterranean worlds.

▓ IRON AGE SEASIDERS

Owain Roberts (2004) points out the complete dearth of direct evidence for Iron Age seagoing vessels in the Atlantic Archipelago, which might be considered rather odd when compared with the relative riches of the Bronze Age. It is clear that seaborne communication did not end, and artefacts of the new metallurgy were as keenly distributed as the old were. Frances Pryor (2004) has suggested that the remarkable Bronze Age boat survivals are due to the specific ritual disposal of artefacts in boggy and watery places in the Bronze Age. This practice appears to continue in the Iron Age (Bradley 1990). Across the Archipelago, there are finds of the ubiquitous log boat. Roberts (2004), although very tentative, proposes that some of the larger examples may have been used at sea. Although oak-hulled craft were described by Julius Caesar as being used by the Veneti in Brittany waters some 2000 years ago, perhaps in the Archipelago the large oak trees required for plank boats became rarer due to the need for clearings for agriculture and settlement. Could it be that in the archipelago the hide-covered boat, the *currach*, comes into its own as the seagoing craft of choice in this period? The *currach's* lightness of construction, an advantage in relation to buoyancy and beaching, means that their survivability in archaeological deposits is significantly poorer than the plank boats (McGrail 2004). Although Wooding (2001) worries that the ubiquity of *currachs* in early Irish texts may be because of their use specifically in penitential voyages at that time, Roberts (2004: 41) finds

> Despite the limits on size, probably about 10m, the curraghs [sic] would have been of outstanding importance from prehistoric through to recent times in maintaining sea connections among the British Isles [Atlantic Archipelago] and with the Continent.

That these sea connections were present is without a doubt, and a variety of craft types probably plied the seaways, although there may have been periods when the intensity and directionality changed.

Over many years, through excavation, survey, assessment of the material indicators and surviving texts, Barry Cunliffe (most notably for our purposes 2001) has provided abundant evidence of such contacts. I do not wish to repeat those details here, but rather wish to consider a couple of points raised by Cunliffe which are examples of interpretations possible through a consideration of maritime prehistory. The first is in regard to the ubiquitous coastal sites on promontories dating to this period in the Atlantic Archipelago and the second and related issue is in regard to the distribution of Celtic languages and how they might link the maritime communities of the western seaways.

During the Iron Age, where the geography was most suitable, typically in the areas bordering the western seaways, cliff-top promontories, headlands and peninsulas become the focus of activity. Usually the promontory was defined by some structure, one or more ditch and bank, or a ditch and stone built wall. The structures crossing the isthmus can be very elaborate or quite simple, but the common feature in each case results in the defining of a space, cut off from the land by a constructed boundary and otherwise surrounded by the sea. Comparisons are often drawn between these sites and other contemporary sites, such as hill forts and duns, typically leading them to being termed 'promontory forts' or 'promontory duns'.

Cunliffe (2001) calls these places 'cliff castles' and notes that although defence would be an understandable function given their location on cliff tops, the indications that many were also occupied do not correspond with their exposed locations. Instead, given the apparent maritime nature of these coast dwellers, Cunliffe suggests that these cliff castles were positioned and defined to make a clear symbolic link between the land and the sea. This was a liminal zone perhaps, where, as a location that more often than not might be a key landmark to mariners, people of the sea and the littoral could come together. Further links along the Atlantic seaways at this time are suggested by the presence of *chevaux-de-frise*, a distinctive feature of stones embedded in the ground to apparently impede the approach to the boundary works by people on foot or on horseback. These features, although most common in the Iberian Peninsula, are found in Wales, Ireland and as far north as Scotland.

The second of Cunliffe's proposals relates to the sharing of language along the Atlantic seaways. Cunliffe opines that given the apparent time depth of maritime contacts along the western seaways, it may be expected that a *lingua franca* would be adopted. This *lingua franca*, perhaps what may be called a trade language, he suggests was what today is called Celtic and which links the same geographical areas in the present day (but see Isaac 2004). Cunliffe is of the opinion that maritime activity would be under the control of elites and that the earlier diversity of languages was replaced by a top-down spread of usage. However, we have already noted in

Chapter 3 how mariners in historic times developed such language skills to cope with the diversity of contacts and this does not have to be elite led.

IRISH SEA/MEDITERRANEAN SEA

At the beginning of the Neolithic, many maritime skills arrived in highly developed form and most probably had their antecedents in the Mediterranean Sea, even perhaps the sailing nursery of the Aegean Sea. On arriving in the Atlantic, these skills needed to be honed to cope with the tides and currents of the ocean. Although not providing an area for primary development, the Irish Sea zone (according to Mackinder the 'Mediterranean Sea' of the Atlantic Archipelago) with an extension through to the Hebrides, once again provides the type of maritime environment in which such new skills could be practiced and developed. Eventually, of course, the skills of the Baltic sailing nursery found their way from the north to meet the influence from the south, allowing for fusion and further developments.

According to Peter Fowler (2004: 92, emphasis mine) the Atlantic Archipelago ought to be regarded as:

> a single archaeological site, fragmented into lots of islands. It is therefore one cultural landscape. This concept is intellectually sustainable, for Britain [and Ireland], Europe's offshore islands, has been extensively busy with people for a long time. They have occupied, hunted over, felled and burnt trees on, farmed in, *communicated across,* and extracted resources from virtually every hectare of the islands' extremely varied terrain since the final stages of the last glaciation 12,000 and more years ago.

I do not wish to argue against Fowler's description of the archaeological history of the Atlantic Archipelago. In particular, as we have seen, I wish to draw attention to the 'communicate across' element of the above quote. This archaeological landscape of islands at various periods can seem divided or extended to parts of the continent and it is the role of people's perception of the sea that has allowed fusion to occur in what otherwise at first sight may be regarded as a hopelessly fragmented landscape.

8

Conclusion – Islands and Histories of the Sea

In this book, I have proposed that islands should be a focus of study in regard to their relations with the sea rather than the apparently circumscribed piece of land they represent. In doing this, I have described four case studies which have provided avenues for exploring such an approach. An archaeology of the sea has much to commend it, but there are some loose ends which require clearing up. First, what specifically do I mean when I talk of 'maritime communities', what role is there for island archaeology in the future, and finally when the land is viewed from the sea what does an archaeology of the sea provide?

◼ COMMUNITIES IN THE FIELD

In Chapter 3, I argued that there was something distinct about people involved in the sea, something which would allow the application of the label 'maritime communities'. These communities are the collections of people for whom I have attempted to establish a framework of their histories through a focus on the sea rather than the land. The maritime prehistories have, of course, been mediated through the present, and in particular through a consideration of literature relating to modern and historical populations for whom the sea was a defining factor, whether or not they actually ventured on it regularly, or even at all. These are people that we may say have 'salt in their blood' in that the sea defines them. It is easy to forget that in the last century and a half, populations with a marine focus have been by-passed and dispersed through the mechanisation of marine technology. Steamships needed fewer ports of call as voyages became more direct and faster. The maritime hearts of urban centres have been ripped out and removed as larger, deeper draft vessels with bulky cargoes required new sites out of town. Container ports need docks closer to deep channels and abundant space for loading and unloading paraphernalia and cargo storage. How then do I envisage the maritime communities of the past?

It is useful, I think, to return to issues raised in Chapter 3 by considering the experience of Roger Just (2000), who, as a young ethnographer in the late 1970s, found in the Ionian Islands of Greece a 'traditional' village on a 'remote' island. Or at least that is what he thought from outward appearances, but he soon found, disconcertingly in regards to his anthropological research, that the majority of people he met were better travelled than he and that the village's 'economy was securely linked to the international world, for the majority of [the village] men of middle age or younger were sailors' (2000: 19). Added to this was the fact that the majority of the villagers had lived in or were linked by kin to the Greek diasporic communities of Australia, South Africa, North America or elsewhere.

Just (2000: 5) had to re-orientate his research to meet the conditions he found, and in the introduction to the resulting book he expresses this with a clarity which nesophiles disappointed by finding the islands of their dreams and imaginings slipping away may find salutatory:

> that my notion of a traditional village was hopelessly misconceived (not because everything had, but because everything is *always* changing) in the end mattered little, for if this is a book about a relatively small, relatively isolated, Greek rural community, part of my purpose now is to show that such communities are, and always have been, anything but removed from the large-scale social processes that have shaped, and continue to shape, the contemporary world.

Just speaks freely of a community, although recognising the long and difficult career the term has had in anthropology. The village community was not the island community, and the villagers held what appears to be a strong animosity to their neighbours in the other urban cluster on the island, but the boundaries were difficult to define. It became clear that kinship was paramount in deciding who was included or excluded from the community. Marriage was the only way of establishing a presence; residence mattered little in the village unless a kinship relationship was established. Such a situation is typical of the Caroline Islands of Micronesia, where kinship and shared clan ancestry maintain community ties over a vast expanse of islands. In the present day, these are more likely to be physically realised through visits and the taking or sending of foodstuffs on the regularly scheduled island-hopping flights from Hawaii to Guam. One has a sense of the normality of this mode of transport as one might use a bus elsewhere, and at each of the ends of the line of flight are diasporic communities taking the consanguineous relationships beyond that of the normal sailing pattern. The community is no less strong due to this as kinship is the tie that binds.

However, when I talk of maritime communities I am not thinking of kin-related groups of people. Anthony Cohen (e.g., 1985) has shown how the boundaries of a community are established by symbolic boundaries, within which each member imagines their presence in the community. Such things as ancestral clan linkages can be used as the past is a resource that may establish some boundaries. One of Cohen's key ethnographic experiences was with a crofting community in the islands of Shetland at the northern end of the Atlantic Archipelago and his imagining of a community appears to be one which is small in scale and very tightly bounded, smaller that is than the island or the modern political boundaries of the region. Cohen points to greetings as one identifier of membership of a community, for example, the type of handshake, the form of kisses and so on, and he does not discuss material forms which might indicate membership. Here I am thinking of the weave, pattern or colour of clothes, such as pullovers, particular styles or placement of tattoos (a long-used tradition in Europe as well as Oceania; see Broodbank 2000 for evidence from the Early Bronze Age Mediterranean), or particular types of jewellery or amulets, such as the 'lucky charms' carried by seafarers in Scotland (Pollard 1999).

The community I conceive as a maritime community is one where such symbolic markers are recognised as affiliation to smaller groupings of people, but also one where either party in the observation will recognise in these materials a shared experience, one linked to the sea. Gerard Delanty (2003) although talking of a different era and imaging different forms of connections does, I think, hit upon something that relates to maritime communities in his defining of contemporary communities as 'communities of communication' where it is, 'organized more like a network, community today is abstract and lacks visibility and unity, and as a result is more an imagined condition than a symbolically shaped reality based on fixed reference points' (2003: 189). In part this helps define the expectations for maritime communities, which are always part of potential networks, whose symbols of the locally imagined community, whether they are physically materialised or based on ancestral and kin connections, are clear, but become more fuzzy in various directions of communication, but as a community of communication the different connections are in this broader community which recognises the shared experience.

In essence, and paradoxically given the term, we can see the sea and links to it in the terms of what Pierre Bourdieu (e.g., 1993) has called a 'field' of cultural production in which there are imagined communities where communication, with potential rhizome-like networks, is the key relationship. Other, symbolic communities are nested within this greater one of the maritime communities. The field is the context in which the individual agent gains experience, that is, the bounds within which *habitus* is both practiced and gained. It is, I argue, in the maritime context that the majority of islanders find the experience which is passed from one generation to the next and creates a maritime community with expectations of communication across broad networks.

THE ARCHAEOLOGY OF ISLANDS

If the maritime and marine environments are the connecting factors which link most people on islands to each other and to coastal communities elsewhere in the world, is there any specific role for the archaeology of islands?

Cyprian Broodbank (2000) thinks island archaeology does not require justification as islands are worthy of study because they are there, a bit like the reason for climbing Mount Everest! He says '[i]sland archaeology is worth doing because islands exist in profusion, and because their archaeology is undeniably fascinating' (2000: 32). So apart from the fact they are there, which in itself does not explain why a sub-discipline of 'island archaeology' is required, their archaeology is fascinating. Can this latter statement really be true of all islands? Some islands have no evidence of human presence whatsoever prior to the modern age (Anderson 2004 notes that of the 25,000 islands in the Pacific, only 1000 have ever been inhabited), and others are covered with industrial complexes and modern cities and I suspect Broodbank does not have these in mind. He appears to be assuming the island aesthetic that goes unchallenged in Western thought, the holiday island image, which is probably easy to maintain in a Mediterranean context. Broodbank goes on to say that the essential nature of island archaeology is 'reason enough, as Pacific archaeologists seem readiest to recognise' (2000: 32). Although in Chapter 5 I have offered an alternative to the island-based archaeology of the Pacific through an archaeology of the sea, most archaeologists in the Pacific have no choice but to work on islands if that is the geographical sphere of their research activity. Unlike the Mediterranean, where for the most part similar archaeology can be found on neighbouring mainlands, this is not possible for the Pacific, and thus there is not a choice. You either work with the archaeology of islands or you go elsewhere and do different research and write different histories.

Broodbank (2000) does recognise that the 'because they are there' model will not satisfy the rigours of a sub-disciplinary definition and provides further justification in that, 'island societies as they once existed have all but vanished, and . . . archaeology is our only avenue into most islands' past most of the time' (2000: 32). This is, of course, ahistorical essentialist claptrap, which the anthropologists of the twentieth century mostly recognised and discarded as discussed in Chapter 2. It is clear that Broodbank does not believe this himself, as he states on the same page that islands 'are tricky, changing places' and we need to capture the 'subtlety and complexity' of each island's history. Clearly, Broodbank is a nesophile and he is trying to justify a passion which defies easy description and is certainly not amenable to developing an analytical answer as to why islands or island societies need to be studied as a separate category.

Scott Fitzpatrick (2004) in introducing a volume of collected essays on the archaeology of islands attempts to tack between notions of islands as 'isolated' or 'connected' in trying to define island archaeology. He offers this definition:

Different groups of people on islands, by virtue of their restricted territory and because they are surrounded by water, developed in at least partial isolation, which influenced how they evolved culturally. Isolation was not solely geographical, but had psychological aspects as well. If we agree that islands have some inherent 'boundary,' whether mental or physical, then we can approach islands as methodologically and theoretically different than continental land masses, although this does not mean that islands were more or less isolated just because they were surrounded by water. (2004: 7)

That this definition is full of provisos is the result in part, I suggest, of using 'isolation' rather than 'connectedness' as the key feature of islands, but also the impossibility of defining a coherent area of study which solely encompasses islands. In Chapter 1, I showed that islands are typified by the fluidity of their boundaries, and if you cannot define the parameters of the supposed focus of your study, then the concept of a sub-discipline immediately looks rather shaky. In providing a summary chapter for Fitzpatrick's volume, Atholl Anderson (2004) warns island archaeologists that they may be going too far in assuming connectedness is a more likely condition of islands than isolation! But here, it seems Anderson is expressing specific and long-held concerns about Polynesian prehistory and provides a suite of examples where isolation appears to best fit the evidence to his mind. He does conclude, however, that '[d]eep isolation was probably not the most frequent situation on prehistoric islands' (2004: 257), and we should probably regard his examples as possible 'exceptions which make the rule'.

Colin Renfrew (2004) in apparently struggling to define island archaeology proposes that a good starting point is to assess whether the island you are on has an associated mainland. If it does not, then you may proceed with the assurance that this is a 'proper' island 'unto itself'. However, a consideration of the relative circumstances of Malta and Gotland is perhaps useful here. Malta is a modern independent nation and an inhabitant does not look to a mainland, as Malta *is* the mainland, a proper situation for island archaeology, or perhaps not. Sicily looms very large to the north of the Malta archipelago. As we have seen in the study of Stoddart and colleagues (1993), in the Neolithic the orientation of the temple architecture is one that indicates strong associations with Sicily, which perhaps at that time was considered by islanders as akin to a mainland. Conversely, Gotland is part of modern Sweden and mainland Sweden is considered the mainland; however, historically it has been part of Denmark. A shift in direction of mainland might be assumed. In prehistory it was likely not part of any bigger federation and the directionality of contacts were as we have seen, at various times, multidirectional; in these cases the island itself would likely be manifested as the mainland. We ought to be aware then that mainlands are more likely political rather than geographical definitions.

What Fitzpatrick (2004) does achieve is an indication of the patterns and processes that islands may be particularly good at illustrating. These are environmental change, colonisation, migration (and demographic change) and interregional interaction.

Here I agree that, in a limited way, islands do provide particular circumstances that can aid us in thinking about issues of colonisation and methods of enhancing the environment in order to sustain human settlement. Although these issues can still be addressed in continental situations, there is a potential clarity of definition achievable in islands (also Renfrew 2004). The impact of humans on island environments is undeniable. Changes are necessary to make a place inhabitable, whether that is the consumption of local resources, the introduction of new ones or a combination of both. As Anderson (2004: 258) points out for the evidence from Caribbean and Pacific islands, even where the source population is farming, after human colonisation there is evidence of the rapid depletion of '[r]esources of high food value . . . these were often flightless birds, colonial-breeding seabirds, shoreline mammals, turtles, large reef fish, molluscs, and so forth.'

Other palaeoenvironmental evidence used as a proxy indicator for island colonisation, such as peaks in charcoal indicating burning or other alterations to the vegetation, is more difficult to interpret as definitely anthropogenic (references in Fitzpatrick 2004; see also Rainbird 2004). Even if identified as anthropogenic in origin, there are still issues of whether this is evidence of visitation rather than inhabitation. Archaeological indicators for earliest settlement have been claimed in many cases, but showing that it really is the earliest settlement of an island is difficult to prove. Non-anthropogenic environmental change may have significant impacts on the archaeology of small islands. Motivations for colonisation of islands can be the subject of investigation and link in with the colonisation of new areas in continental situations and for the migration of peoples, and the development of diasporic communities. All of these have their continental equivalents but may be more apparent in island situations, although, equally, they may not. Beginning a study of islands with isolation in mind, even 'relative isolation', will undoubtedly affect the outcome of the research. Islands will have a role to play in line with the archaeology from elsewhere.

But islands are much more important than that. Islands are most important for archaeological study because, as we have seen, they are so embedded in the myths and dreams of Western consciousness that in studying island histories archaeologists can challenge some of the fundamental social and political myths of our time. Here I follow John Terrell (2004), who has pointed out that the assumptions underlying notions that island populations are isolated and in that isolation may evolve peculiar traits, is the same as the one which believes that there are distinct 'cultures', 'peoples', 'societies' and I would add 'races' in its most fundamental form. If we can show that the supposedly most bounded pieces of land on the Earth were some of the most connected, leading to the diverse connections expected of maritime communities, then island studies will have served a role in bringing a notion of common humanity, one which brings a diversity of social and biological histories to the fore. Individual islands studied as microcosms will not do this. As Terrell (2004: 206) says, '[i]slands invite us to discover not only what has been happening on them, but also what has been happening between them.'

One of the stumbling blocks to a greater acceptance of the potentialities of the connectedness expected in maritime prehistories is the spectre of diffusionism. As models of contact and migration became replaced by other paradigms, both processual and post-processual in the last three decades of the twentieth century, distaste for accepting any form of diffusion of ideas, technology or people came to the fore. Why, archaeologists asked, should we have to look to a distant elsewhere in order to explain local history? But within a maritime context we do not have to accept that the direction was one way. As we have seen in Chapter 2, post-colonial studies have shown us that contact is a two-way process; all parties to encounters may be changed by the experience. We also have to accept the studies which show that objects can become incorporated into local contexts in ways that bear little similarity to how they were perceived in their point of origin (e.g., Thomas 1991; Miller 1994). We also have to accept that artefacts have life histories of their own and that these biographies reflect the mutability of solid things (Appadurai 1986; Marshall and Gosden 1999). Finally, we no longer need to believe that all innovation derives from external sources and that expectations of contact can lead to change, whether that be in modifying artefacts to enhance exchange opportunities (e.g., Torrence 1993) or providing attractors perhaps in port facilities, or temples and monuments as I have proposed for Malta and Pohnpei, for example. Reducing or repelling contacts can also lead to innovation as suggested in the classical story of Archimedes of Syracuse pointing shiny metal discs so as to deflect the sun and set fire to the wooden ships of the attacking Roman fleet.

■ THE ARCHAEOLOGIES OF THE SEAS

We now have the knowledge to hand which should allow us to exorcise the spectre of diffusionism. In its place accepting that contacts, in perhaps multiple directions, create a rhizome-like web across the unstriated space of oceans and seas, does not lead to unthoughtful adoption of external ideas and objects, does not require us to assume large migrationary movements of people, and does not lead to a loss of local identity. Indeed, we can reverse much of this by saying, in a positive sense, contacts lead to the innovative use of ideas and objects through application of local experience. People of maritime circumstances engage with outsiders socially, and continuously incorporate elements of this contact into their own populace, and through contact and exchanges create a distinct community identity located historically on sea and land.

It has not been my intention in this book to romanticise the view of seafaring in prehistory. I am well aware of the inherent dangers of activities at sea. My father, a marine fisherman and merchant seaman at various times in his life, would comfort my nervous mother before a flight with the truism 'more people die at sea'. This I take as a given and indeed this really gets us to the essence of what this book is about, which is, those who live by the sea take on the fusion, fluidity and flux characteristic of the sea, whether their land base is an island or continent.

References

Anderson, A. 2000 Slow boats from China: issues in the prehistory of Indo-Pacific seafaring. In S. O'Connor and P. Veth (eds.) *East of Wallace's Line: Studies of past and present maritime cultures of the Indo-Pacific region. Modern Quaternary Research in Southeast Asia*, 16. 13–50. A.A. Balkema: Rotterdam.

Anderson, A. 2003 Entering uncharted waters: models of initial colonization in Polynesia. In M. Rockman and J. Steele (eds.) *Colonization of Unfamiliar Landscapes: The archaeology of adaptation*. 169–189. Routledge: London.

Anderson, A. 2004 Islands of ambivalence. In S. Fitzpatrick (ed.) *Voyages of Discovery: The archaeology of islands*. 251–273. Praeger: Westport, Conn.

Appadurai, A. (ed.) 1986 *The Social Life of Things: Commodities in cultural perspective*. Cambridge University Press: Cambridge.

Armit, I. 2003 The drowners: permanence and transience in the Hebridean Neolithic. In I. Armit, E. Murphy, E. Nelis and D. Simpson (eds.) *Neolithic Settlement in Ireland and Western Britain*. 93–100. Oxbow: Oxford.

Ayres, W. S. 2002 Island archaeology and issues of political centralization: Micronesian evidence. In W. Waldren and J. Ensenyat (eds.) *World Islands in Prehistory: International insular investigations*. 57–67. *British Archaeological Reports International Series* 1095.

Bahn, P. and Flenley, J. 1992 *Easter Island, Earth Island.* Thames and Hudson: London.

Ballard, C., Bradley, R., Nordenborg, L. and Wilson, M. 2003 The ship as symbol in the prehistory of Scandinavia and Southeast Asia. *World Archaeology* 35: 385–403.

Barratt, G. 1988 *H.M.S. Centurion at Tinian, 1742: the ethnographic and historic records. Micronesian Archaeological Survey Report,* 26. Historic Preservation Office: Saipan.

Bauer, B. S. and Standish, C. 2001 *Ritual and Pilgrimage in the Ancient Andes: The islands of the sun and moon.* University of Texas Press: Austin.

Bellwood, P. 1997a *Prehistory of the Indo-Malaysian Archipelago.* 2nd edition. University of Hawaii Press: Honolulu.

Bellwood, P. 1997b Taiwan and the prehistory of the Austronesian-speaking people. *The Review of Archaeology,* Fall: 39–48.

Berg, M. L. 1992 Yapese politics, Yapese money and the *Sawei* tribute network before World War I. *Journal of Pacific History* 27: 150–164.

Björk, N. 2003 Neolithic society in eastern Sweden: segmentary, virilocal and animistic? In J. Rönnby (ed.) *By the Water: Archaeological perspectives on human strategies around the Baltic.* 11–36. *Södertörn Academic Studies,* 17.

Bourdieu, P. 1993 *The Field of Cultural Production: Essays on art and literature.* Polity: Cambridge.

Bowen, E. G. 1969 *Saints, Seaways and Settlements in Celtic Lands.* University of Wales Press: Cardiff.

Bowen, E. G. 1970 Britain and the British seas. In D. Moore (ed.) *The Irish Sea Province in Archaeology and History.* 13–28. Cambrian Archaeological Association: Cardiff.

Bowen, E. G. 1972 *Britain and the Western Seaways.* Thames and Hudson: London.

Bradley, R. 1990 *The Passage of Arms: An archaeological analysis of prehistoric hoards and votive offerings.* Cambridge University Press: Cambridge.

Bradley, R. 1997 *Rock Art and the Prehistory of Atlantic Europe: Signing the land.* Routledge: London.

Bradley, R. and Edmonds, M. 1993 *Interpreting the Axe Trade: Production and exchange in Neolithic Britain.* Cambridge University Press: Cambridge.

Branigan, K. and Foster, P. 2002 *Barra and the Bishop's Isle: Living on the margin.* Tempus: Stroud.

Braudel, F. 1972 *The Mediterranean and the Mediterranean World in the Age of Philip II.* Vol. 1. 2nd edition. Translated by S. Reynolds. Collins: London.

Broodbank, C. 1999a The insularity of island archaeologists: comments on Rainbird's "Islands out of time". *Journal of Mediterranean Archaeology* 12: 235–239.

Broodbank, C. 1999b Colonization and configuration in the insular Neolithic of the Aegean. In P. Halstead (ed.) *Neolithic Society in Greece. Sheffield Studies in Aegean Archaeology*, 2. 15–41. Sheffield Academic Press: Sheffield.

Broodbank, C. 2000 *An Island Archaeology of the Early Cyclades.* Cambridge University Press: Cambridge.

Broodbank, C. and Strasser, T. F. 1991 Migrant farmers and the Neolithic colonization of Crete. *Antiquity* 65: 233–245.

Buck, P. H. (Te Rangi Hiroa) 1938 *Vikings of the Sunrise.* Lippincott: Philadelphia.

Burenhult, G. 1986 *Speglingar av det Förflutna.* Wiken: Höganäs.

Burenhult, G. 2002 The grave-field at Ajvide. In G. Burenhult (ed.) *Remote Sensing, Vol. II: Archaeological investigations, remote sensing case studies and osteo-anthropological studies.* 31–172. *Stockholm University Theses and Papers in North-European Archaeology*, 13b.

Burrow, S. 1999 Neither east nor west: a social history of the Manx Neolithic. In P. J. Davey (ed.) *Recent Archaeological Research on the Isle of Man.* 27–38. *British Archaeological Reports British Series*, 278.

Burström, M. 1996 Other generations' interpretation and use of the past: the case of the picture stones on Gotland. *Current Swedish Archaeology* 4: 21–40.

Capelle, T. 1995 Bronze-Age stone ships. In O. Crumlin-Pedersen and B. M. Thye (eds.) *The Ship as Symbol in Prehistoric and Medieval Scandinavia.* 71–75. *Publications of the National Museum (Copenhagen), Studies in Archaeology and History*, 1.

Carlsson, D. 1991 Harbours and trading places on Gotland AD 600–1000. In O. Crumlin-Pedersen (ed.) *Aspects of Maritime Scandinavia AD 200–1200.* 145–158. *Proceedings of the Nordic Seminar on Maritime Aspects of Archaeology, Roskilde, 13–15 March 1989.*

Carver, M. 1990 Pre-Viking traffic in the North Sea. In S. McGrail (ed.) *Maritime Celts, Frisians and Saxons. CBA Research Report*, 71. 117–125. Council for British Archaeology: York.

Castagnino Berlinghieri, E. F. 2002 New contributions to the study of the Neolithic sea/landscape and human interaction on the Aeolian Islands (Sicily, Italy). In W. Waldren and J. Ensenyat (eds.) *World Islands in Prehistory: International insular investigations.* 217–232. *British Archaeological Reports International Series* 1095.

Castagnino Berlinghieri, E. F. 2003 *The Aeolian Islands, crossroads of Mediterranean maritime routes: a survey on their maritime archaeology and topography from the prehistoric to Roman periods. British Archaeological Reports International Series* 1181.

Cazzella, A. 2002 From the beginnings of food production to early forms of social stratification. In B. Cunliffe, W. Davies and C. Renfrew (eds.)

Archaeology: The widening debate. 414–438. British Academy/Oxford University Press: Oxford.

Chapman, H. P. and Chapman, P. R. 2005 Seascapes and landscapes – the siting of the Ferriby boat finds in the context of prehistoric pilotage. *The International Journal of Nautical Archaeology* 34: 43–50.

Cherry, J. F. 1981 Pattern and process in the earliest colonization of the Mediterranean islands. *Proceedings of the Prehistoric Society* 47: 41–68.

Cherry, J. F. 1990 The first colonization of the Mediterranean islands: a review of recent research. *Journal of Mediterranean Archaeology* 3: 145–221.

Cherry, J. F. 2004 Mediterranean island prehistory: what's different and what's new? In S. Fitzpatrick (ed.) *Voyages of Discovery: The archaeology of islands.* 233–248. Praeger: Westport, Conn.

Clark, J. G. D. 1977 The economic context of dolmens and passage-graves in Sweden. In V. Markotic (ed.) *Ancient Europe and the Mediterranean: Studies presented in honour of Hugh Hencken.* 35–49. Aris and Phillips: Warminster.

Clark, P. 2004a Discussion. In P. Clark (ed.) *The Dover Bronze Age Boat.* 305–330. English Heritage: London.

Clark, P. 2004b The Dover Boat ten years after its discovery. In P. Clark (ed.) *The Dover Bronze Age Boat in Context: Society and water transport in prehistoric Europe.* 1–12. Oxbow: Oxford.

Clarke, M. 1952 *For the Term of His Natural Life.* Oxford University Press: Oxford.

Clébert, J-P. 1964 *The Gypsies.* Vista: London.

Clifford, J. 1988 *The Predicament of Culture: Twentieth century ethnography, literature, and art.* Harvard University Press: Cambridge, Mass.

Clifford, J. 1997 *Routes: Travels and translation in the late twentieth century.* Harvard University Press: Cambridge, Mass.

Clifford, J. and Marcus, G. (eds.) 1986 *Writing Culture: The poetics and politics of ethnography.* University of California Press: Berkeley.

Coates, J. 2005 The Bronze Age Ferriby boats: seagoing ships or estuary ferry boats? *The International Journal of Nautical Archaeology* 34: 38–42.

Cohen, A. 1985 *The Symbolic Construction of Community.* Routledge: London.

Coleman, S. and Elsner, J. 1995 *Pilgrimage: Past and present.* British Museum Press: London.

Connolly, B. and Anderson, R. 1989 *First Contact: New Guinea's Highlanders encounter the outside world.* Penguin: Harmondsworth.

Cooney, G. 2004 Neolithic worlds; islands in the Irish Sea. In V. Cummings and C. Fowler (eds.) *The Neolithic of the Irish Sea: Materiality and traditions of practice.* 145–159. Oxbow: Oxford.

Cooney, G. and Mandel, S. 1998 *The Irish Stone Axe Project, Monograph 1.* Wordwell: Dublin.

Craib, J. L. nd. The Beaked Adze in Oceania: implications for late prehistoric contacts within the western Pacific. MS in possession of author.

Crowley, T. 1994 Proto who drank kava. In A. Pawley and M. Ross (eds.) *Austronesian Terminologies: Continuity and change*. 87–100. *Pacific Linguistics C–127*. Department of Linguistics, Research School of Pacific and Asian Studies, Australian National University: Canberra.

Csordas, T. J. 1999 The body's career in anthropology. In H. L. Moore (ed.) *Anthropological Theory Today*. 172–205. Polity: Cambridge.

Cummings, V. and Fowler, C. 2004 Introduction. In V. Cummings and C. Fowler (eds.) *The Neolithic of the Irish Sea: Materiality and traditions of practice*. 1–8. Oxbow: Oxford.

Cunliffe, B. 2001 *Facing the Ocean: The Atlantic and its peoples, 8000 BC–AD 1500*. Oxford University Press: Oxford.

Curet, L. A. 2004 Island archaeology and units of analysis in the study of ancient Caribbean societies. In S. Fitzpatrick (ed.) *Voyages of Discovery: The archaeology of islands*. 187–201. Praeger: Westport, Conn.

Daniel, G. 1941 The dual nature of the megalithic colonisation of Europe. *Proceedings of the Prehistoric Society* 7: 1–49.

Darvill, T. 2001 *Billown Neolithic Landscape Project. Sixth Report: 2000*. Bournemouth University and Manx National Heritage: Bournemouth and Douglas.

Darvill, T. 2004 Tales of the land, tales of the sea: people and presence in the Neolithic of Man and beyond. In V. Cummings and C. Fowler (eds.) *The Neolithic of the Irish Sea: Materiality and traditions of practice*. 46–54. Oxbow: Oxford.

Dathorne, O. R. 1996 *Asian Voyages. Two thousand years of constructing the other*. Bergin and Garvey: Westport, Conn.

Davey, P. 2004 The Isle of Man: central or marginal in the Neolithic of the northern Irish Sea. In V. Cummings and C. Fowler (eds.) *The Neolithic of the Irish Sea: Materiality and traditions of practice*. 129–144. Oxbow: Oxford.

Davidson, J. M. 1988 Archaeology in Micronesia since 1965: past achievements and future prospects. *New Zealand Journal of Archaeology* 10: 83–100.

Defoe, D. 1965 *Robinson Crusoe*. Penguin: Harmondsworth.

Delanty, G. 2003 *Community*. Routledge: London.

Deleuze, G. 2004 *Desert Islands and Other Texts 1953–1975*. (Edited by D. Lapoujade. Translated by M. Taormina). Semiotext(e): Los Angeles.

Deleuze, G. and Guattari, F. 1988 *A Thousand Plateaus: Capitalism and schizophrenia*. (Translated by B. Massumi). Athlone: London.

Dening, G. 1972 The geographical knowledge of the Polynesians and the nature of inter-island contact. In J. Golson (ed.) *Polynesian Navigation:*

A symposium on Andrew Sharp's theory of accidental voyages. 3rd edition. 102–153. Polynesian Society/Reed: Wellington.

Dening, G. 1980 *Islands and Beaches. Discourses on a silent land: Marquesas 1774–1880*. Melbourne University Press: Melbourne.

Dening, G. 1992 *Mr Bligh's Bad Language: Passion, power and theatre on the Bounty*. Cambridge University Press: Cambridge.

Dening, G. 1996 Voices from the beach. In R. Gibson (ed.) *Exchanges: Cross-cultural encounters in Australia and the Pacific*. 163–184. Historic Houses Trust of New South Wales: Sydney.

Dening, G. 2003 Afterword. In R. Edmond and V. Smith (eds.) *Islands in History and Representation*. 203–206. Routledge: London.

Dennell, R. 1983 *European Economic Prehistory*. Academic Press: London.

Doumas, C. 2004 Aegean islands and islanders. In J. Cherry, C. Scarre and S. Shennan (eds.) *Explaining Social Change: Studies in honour of Colin Renfrew*. 215–226. McDonald Institute Monographs: Cambridge.

Doyle, A. C., Sir 1996 *The Hound of the Baskervilles*. Penguin: Harmondsworth.

Dumville, D. N. 2002 The north Atlantic monastic thalassocracy: sailing the desert in early medieval insular spirituality. In B. E. Crawford (ed.) *The Papar in the North Atlantic: Environment and History. The 'Papar' Project, Vol. 1. St. John's House Papers, 10*. 121–131. Committee for Dark Age Studies, University of St. Andrews: St. Andrews.

Dwyer, P. D., Just, R. and Minnegal, M. 2003 A sea of small names: Fishers and their boats in Victoria, Australia. *Anthropological Forum* 13: 5–26.

Eade, J. and Sallnow, M. J. 1991 *Contesting the Sacred: The anthropology of Christian pilgrimage*. Routledge: London.

Ellmers, D. 1995 Valhalla and the Gotland stones. In O. Crumlin-Pedersen and B. M. Thye (eds.) *The Ship as Symbol in Prehistoric and Medieval Scandinavia*. 165–171. *Publications of the National Museum (Copenhagen), Studies in Archaeology and History*, 1.

Eriksen, T. H. 1993 In which sense do cultural islands exist? *Social Anthropology* 1: 133–147.

Evans, J. D. 1971 *The Prehistoric Antiquities of the Maltese Islands: A survey*. Athlone: London.

Evans, J. D. 1973 Islands as laboratories for the study of cultural process. In C. Renfrew (ed.) *The Explanation of Culture Change: Models in prehistory*. 517–520. Duckworth: London.

Evans, J. D. 1977 Island archaeology in the Mediterranean: problems and opportunities. *World Archaeology* 9: 12–26.

Finney, B. 1992 *From Sea to Space – The Macmillan Brown Lectures*. Massey University: Palmerston North.

Finney, B. 1998 Nautical cartography and traditional navigation in Oceania. In D. Woodward and G. M. Lewis (eds.) *The History of Cartography, Volume 2, Book Three, Cartography in the Traditional African, American, Arctic, Australian, and Pacific Societies.* 443–492. University of Chicago Press: Chicago.

Fitzpatrick, S. 2004 Synthesizing island archaeology. In S. Fitzpatrick (ed.) *Voyages of Discovery: The archaeology of islands.* 3–18. Praeger: Westport, Conn.

Flanagan, R. 1996 Anti-museum: the case of the Strahan Wharf Centre. In S. Hunt (ed.) *Sites. Nailing the Debate: Archaeology and interpretation in museums.* 179–197. Museum of Sydney: Sydney.

Flannery, T. 1994 *The Future Eaters.* Reed: Sydney.

Fleming, A. 2005 *St. Kilda and the Wider World: Tales of an iconic island.* Windgather Press: Macclesfield.

Flenley, J. and Bahn, P. 2003 *The Enigmas of Easter Island.* Oxford University Press: Oxford.

Forster, J. R. 1996 [1778] *Observations Made During a Voyage Around the World.* New edition edited by N. Thomas, H. Guest and M. Dettelbach. University of Hawaii Press: Hawaii.

Fowler, P. 2004 *Landscapes for the World: Conserving a global heritage.* Windgather: Macclesfield.

Fox, A. 1995 Tin ingots from Bigbury Bay. *Proceedings of the Devon Archaeological Society* 53: 11–23.

Fox, H. 2001 *The Evolution of the Fishing Village: Landscape and society along the South Devon coast. Leicester Explorations on Local History,* 1. Leopard's Head Press: Oxford.

Gell, A. 1985 How to read a map: remarks on the practical logic of navigation. *Man* (NS) 20: 271–286.

Gell, A. 1995 The language of the forest: landscape and phonological iconism in Umeda. In E. Hirsch and M. O'Hanlon (eds.) *The Anthropology of Landscape: Perspectives on place and space.* 232–254. Oxford University Press: Oxford.

Gibson, R. 1994 Ocean settlement. *Meanjin* 4: 665–678.

Gillett, R. 1987 *Traditional Tuna Fishing: A study at Satawal, central Caroline Islands. Bishop Museum Bulletin in Anthropology,* 1.

Gillis, J. R. 2003 Taking history offshore: Atlantic islands in European minds, 1400–1800. In R. Edmond and V. Smith (eds.) *Islands in History and Representation.* 19–31. Routledge: London.

Gladwin, T. 1970 *East Is a Big Bird.* Harvard University Press: Cambridge, Mass.

Goodenough, W. H. 1986 Sky world and this world: the place of *Kachaw* in Micronesian cosmology. *American Anthropologist* 88: 551–568.

Gosden, C. 2001 Making sense: archaeology and aesthetics. *World Archaeology* 33: 163–167.

Grima, R. 2001 An iconography of insularity: a cosmological interpretation of some images and spaces in the late Neolithic temples of Malta. *Papers from the Institute of Archaeology* 12: 48–65.

Hage, P. and Harary, F. 1991 *Exchange in Oceania: A graph theoretical analysis.* Clarendon Press: Oxford.

Halliburton, M. 2002 Rethinking anthropological studies of the body: *Manas* and *Bōdham* in Kerala. *American Anthropologist* 104: 1123–1134.

Hamilakis, Y. 2001 Art and the representation of the past: commentary. *Journal of the Royal Anthropological Institute* 7: 153–154.

Hamilakis, Y. 2002 'The other Parthenon': antiquity and national memory at Makronisos. *Journal of Modern Greek Studies* 20: 307–338.

Hamilakis, Y. forthcoming *The Archaeology of the Senses.* Cambridge University Press: Cambridge.

Hardy, T. 1986 *The Well-Beloved.* Oxford University Press: Oxford.

Harvey, D. 1990 *The Condition of Postmodernity.* Blackwell: Oxford.

Hather, J. and Kirch, P. V. 1991 Prehistoric sweet potato (*Ipomoea batatas*) from Mangaia Island, Central Polynesia. *Antiquity* 65: 887–893.

Hauʻofa, E. 1975 Anthropology and Pacific islanders. *Oceania* 45: 283–289.

Hauʻofa, E. 1993 Our sea of islands. In E. Waddell, V. Naidu, and E. Hauʻofa, (eds.) *A New Oceania: Rediscovering our sea of islands.* 2–16. University of the South Pacific Press: Fiji.

Held, S. O. 1990 Islands in space: quantification and simulation in theoretical island archaeology. Unpublished TAG 90 Session Abstracts, 36–37.

Held, S. O. 1993 Insularity as a modifier of culture change: the case of prehistoric Cyprus. *Bulletin of the American Schools of Oriental Research* 292: 25–33.

Hodges, R. 1982 *Dark Age Economics.* Duckworth: London.

Horden, P. and Purcell, N. 2000 *Corrupting Sea: A study in Mediterranean history.* Blackwell: Oxford.

Horn, W., White Marshall, J. and Rourke, G. D. 1990 *The Forgotten Hermitage of Skellig Michael.* University of California Press: Berkeley.

Howes, D. 2003 *Sensual Relations: Engaging the senses in culture and social theory.* University of Michigan Press: Ann Arbor.

Hunter, J. R. 1994 'Maritime culture': notes from the land. *The International Journal of Nautical Archaeology* 23: 261–264.

Hunter-Anderson, R. L. and Zan, Y. (Goʻopsan) 1996 Demystifying the *Sawei*, a traditional interisland exchange system. *ISLA: A Journal of Micronesian Studies* 4: 1–45.

Ihde, D. 1993 *Postphenomenology: Essays in the postmodern context.* Northwestern University Press: Evanston, Ill.

Ingold, T. 2000 *The Perception of the Environment: Essays in livelihood, dwelling and skill.* Routledge: London.

Irwin, G. 1992 *The Prehistoric Exploration and Colonisation of the Pacific.* Cambridge University Press: Cambridge.

Irwin, G. 2000 No man is an island: the importance of context in the study of the colonisation and settlement of the Pacific Islands. In A. Anderson and T. Murray (eds) *Australian Archaeologist: Collected papers in honour of Jim Allen.* 393–411. Coombs Academic Publishing, The Australian National University: Canberra.

Isaac, G. R. 2004 The nature and origins of the Celtic languages: Atlantic seaways and other paralinguistic misapprehensions. *Studia Celtica* 38: 49–58.

Jacobsen, T. W. 1976 17,000 years of Greek prehistory. *Scientific American* 234(6): 76–89.

Jolly, M. 1996 Desire, difference and disease: sexual and venereal exchanges on Cook's voyages in the Pacific. In R. Gibson (ed.) *Exchanges: Cross-cultural encounters in Oceania.* 185–217. Museum of Sydney: Sydney.

Jolly, M. 2001 On the edge? Deserts, oceans, islands. *The Contemporary Pacific* 13: 417–466.

Jones, P. L. 2005 New dawn on early Cyprus. *Antiquity* 79: 450–454.

Jones, R. M. 1977 The Tasmanian paradox. In R. V. S. Wright (ed.) *Stone Tools as Cultural Markers: Change, evolution and complexity.* 189–204. Australian Institute of Aboriginal Studies: Canberra.

Jones, T. L. and Klar, K. A. 2005 Diffusionism reconsidered: linguistic and archaeological evidence for prehistoric Polynesian contact with southern California. *American Antiquity* 70: 457–484.

Jonsonn, M. and Lindquist, S-O. 1997 *Gateway to Gotland.* (English Trans. by J. Tate). Gotlands Fornsal: Visby.

Just, R. 2000 *A Greek Island Cosmos: Kinship and community on Meganisi.* James Currey: Oxford.

Karolle, B. G. 1993 *Atlas of Micronesia.* 2nd edition. Bess Press: Honolulu.

Keegan, W. F. 1999 Comment on Paul Rainbird "Islands out of time: towards a critique of island archaeology". *Journal of Mediterranean Archaeology* 12: 255–258.

Keegan, W. F. and Diamond, J. 1987 Colonization of islands by humans: a biogeographical perspective. In M.B. Schiffer (ed.), *Advances in Archaeological Method and Theory* 10: 49–92. Academic Press: San Diego.

Kirby, D. and Hinkkanen, M. 2000 *The Baltic and the North Seas.* Routledge: London.

Kirch, P. V. 1984 *The Evolution of the Polynesian Chiefdoms.* Cambridge University Press: Cambridge.

Kirch, P. V. 1997 Microcosmic histories: island perspectives on 'global' change. *American Anthropologist* 99: 30–42.

Kirch, P. V. 2000 *On the Road of the Winds: An archaeological history of the Pacific Islands before European contact.* University of California Press: Berkeley.

Kirch, P. V. and Green, R. C. 2001 *Hawaiki, Ancestral Polynesia: An essay in historical anthropology.* Cambridge University Press: Cambridge.

Kohn, T. 2002 Imagining islands. In W. Waldren and J. Ensenyat (eds.) *World Islands in Prehistory: International insular investigations.* 39–43. British Archaeological Reports International Series 1095.

Kristiansen, K. 1998 Centre and periphery in Bronze Age Scandinavia. In K. Kristiansen and M. Rowlands *Social Transformations in Archaeology: Global and local perspectives.* 268–286. Routledge: London.

Kuklick, H. 1996 Islands in the Pacific: Darwinian biogeography and British anthropology. *American Ethnologist* 23: 611–638.

Lape, P. V. 2004 The isolation metaphor in island archaeology. In S. Fitzpatrick (ed.) *Voyages of Discovery: The archaeology of islands.* 223–232. Praeger: Westport, Conn.

Lebot, V. 1991 *Kava (Piper methysticum* Forst. f.): The Polynesian dispersal. In P. A. Cox and S. A. Barnack (eds.) *Islands, Plants, and Polynesians: An introduction to Polynesian ethnobotany.* 169–201. Dioscorides: Portland.

Lebot, V., Merlin, M. and Lindstrom, L. 1992 *Kava: The Pacific Drug.* Yale University Press: New Haven.

Lee, R. 1998 The socio-economic and demographic characteristics of port cities: a typology for comparative analysis? *Urban History* 25: 147–172.

Lewis, D. 1994 *We, the Navigators: The ancient art of landfinding in the Pacific.* 2nd edition. University of Hawaii Press: Honolulu.

Lindqvist, C. and Possnert, G. 1997 The subsistence economy and diet at Jakobs/Ajvide and Stora Förvar, Eksta Parish and other prehistoric dwelling and burial sites on Gotland in long-term perspective. In G. Burenhult (ed.) *Remote Sensing, Vol. I: Osteo-anthropological, economic, environmental and technical analyses.* 29–90. Stockholm University Theses and Papers in North-European Archaeology, 13a.

Lindqvist, C. and Possnert, G. 1999 The first seal hunter families on Gotland: on the Mesolithic occupation in the Stora Förvar Cave. *Current Swedish Archaeology* 7: 65–87.

MacArthur, R. H. and Wilson, E. O. 1967 *The Theory of Island Biogeography. Monographs in Population Biology,* 1. Princeton University Press: Princeton.

McGrail, S. 1990 Boats and boatmanship in the late prehistoric southern North Sea and Channel region. In S. McGrail (ed.) *Maritime Celts, Frisians and Saxons.* 32–48. *Council for British Archaeology Research Report,* 71.

McGrail, S. 2004 North-west European sea-going boats before AD 400. In P. Clark (ed.) *The Dover Bronze Age Boat in Context: Society and water transport in prehistoric Europe.* 51–66. Oxbow: Oxford.

McGrane, B. 1989 *Beyond Anthropology: Society and the Other.* Columbia University Press: New York.

McKechnie, R. 2002 Islands of indifference. In W. Waldren and J. Ensenyat (eds.) *World Islands in Prehistory: International insular investigations.* 127–134. *British Archaeological Reports International Series* 1095.

McNiven, I. 2003 Saltwater people: spiritscapes, maritime rituals and the archaeology of Australian indigenous seascapes. *World Archaeology* 35: 329–349.

Magro Conti, J. 1999 Aggression and defence in prehistoric Malta. In A. Mifsud and C. Savona Ventura (eds.) *Facets of Maltese Prehistory.* 191–205. Prehistoric Society of Malta: Mosta.

Malinowski, B. 1922 *The Argonauts of the Western Pacific.* Routledge: London.

Malone, C. and Stoddart, S. 2004 Towards an island of mind? In J. Cherry, C. Scarre and S. Shennan (eds.) *Explaining Social Change: Studies in honour of Colin Renfrew.* 93–102. McDonald Institute Monographs: Cambridge.

Marsden, P. 2004 Reconstructing the Dover boat. In P. Clark (ed.) *The Dover Bronze Age Boat in Context: Society and water transport in prehistoric Europe.* 17–19. Oxbow: Oxford.

Marshall, Y. and Gosden, C. (eds.) 1999 The cultural biography of objects. *World Archaeology* 31(2): 169–178.

Mead, M. 1942 *Growing up in New Guinea.* Penguin: Harmondsworth.

Melville, H. 1967 *Moby Dick.* Norton: New York.

Mercer, R. J. 2003 The early farming settlement of south western England in the Neolithic. In I. Armit, E. Murphy, E. Nelis and D. Simpson (eds.) *Neolithic Settlement in Ireland and Western Britain.* 56–70. Oxbow: Oxford.

Miller, D. 1994 *Modernity: An ethnographic approach.* Berg: Oxford.

Mitchell, P. 2004 Towards a comparative archaeology of Africa's islands. *Journal of African Archaeology* 2: 229–250.

Montin, K. 1994 The seaman's conception of himself. In S. Fisher (ed.) *Man and the Environment. Exeter Maritime Studies,* 9. 199–209. Exeter University Press: Exeter.

Moorehead, A. 1966 *The Fatal Impact: An account of the invasion of the South Pacific.* Hamilton: London.

More, T. 1923 *Utopia.* Translated G. Richards. Blackwell: Oxford.

Morwood, M. J., Aziz, F., O'Sullivan, P., Nasruddin, Hobbs, D. R. and Raza, A. 1999 Archaeological and palaeontological research in central Flores, east Indonesia: results of fieldwork 1997–98. *Antiquity* 73: 273–286.

Morwood, M. J., Soejono, R. P., Roberts, R. G., Sutikna, T., Turney, C., West-away, K., Rink, W., Zhao, J., van den Bergh, G., Rokus Awe Due, Hobbs, D., Moore, M., Bird, M. and Fifield, L. 2004 Archaeology and age of a new hominin from Flores in eastern Indonesia. *Nature* 431: 1087–1091.

Moss, M. L. 2004 Island societies are not always insular: Tingit territories in the Alexander Archipelago and the adjacent Alaskan mainland. In S. Fitzpatrick (ed.) *Voyages of Discovery: The archaeology of islands.* 165–183. Praeger: Westport, Conn.

Nayling, N. and Caseldine, A. 1997 *Excavations at Caldicot, Gwent: Bronze Age palaeochannels in the lower Nedern Valley. Council for British Archaeology Research Report*, 108.

O'Loughlin, T. 1997 Living in the Ocean. In C. Bourke (ed.) *Studies in the Cult of Saint Columba.* 11–23. Four Courts Press: Dublin.

O'Loughlin, T. 1999 Distant islands: the topography of holiness in the *Navigatio Sancti Brendani*. In M. Glasscoe (ed.) *The Medieval Mystical Tradition. England, Ireland and Wales.* 1–20. D.S. Brewer: Woodbridge.

O'Loughlin, T. 2000 *Journeys on the Edges: The Celtic tradition.* Darton, Long-man and Todd: London.

Okely, J. 1983 *The Traveller-Gypsies.* Cambridge University Press: Cambridge.

Olsson, L. and Öhrman, R. 1996 *Gotland – Past and Present.* Revised edition. Gotlands Läromedelscentral: Visby.

Österholm, I. 2002 The pattern of stone age settlements on Gotland. In G. Burenhult (ed.) *Remote Sensing, Vol. II : Archaeological investigations, remote sensing case studies and osteo-anthropological studies.* 219–242. *Stockholm University Theses and Papers in North-European Archaeology*, 13b.

Österholm, S. 2002 Boats in prehistory – report on an archaeological experiment. In G. Burenhult (ed.) *Remote Sensing, Vol. II : Archaeological investigations, remote sensing case studies and osteo-anthropological studies.* 323–342. *Stockholm University Theses and Papers in North-European Archaeology*, 13b.

Pagden, A. 1993 *European Encounters with the New World.* Yale University Press: New Haven.

Parker, A. J. 1999 A maritime cultural landscape: the port of Bristol in the Middle Ages. *The International Journal of Nautical Archaeology* 28: 323–342.

Parker, A. J. 2001 Maritime landscapes. *Landscapes* 1: 22–41.

Parker Pearson, M. 2004 Island prehistories: a view of Orkney from South Uist. In J. Cherry, C. Scarre and S. Shennan (eds.) *Explaining Social Change: Studies in honour of Colin Renfrew.* 127–140. McDonald Institute Monographs: Cambridge.

Patton, M. 1996 *Islands in Time: Island sociogeography and Mediterranean pre-history.* Routledge: London.

Peiser, B. 2005 From genocide to ecocide: the rape of Rapa Nui. *Energy and Environment* 16: 513–539.

Perlès, C. 2001 *The Early Neolithic of Greece.* Cambridge University Press: Cambridge.

Petersen, G. 1990a *Lost in the weeds: Theme and variation in Pohnpei political mythology. Center for Pacific Island Studies, University of Hawai'i, Occasional Paper,* 35.

Petersen, G. 1990b Some overlooked complexities in the study of Pohnpei social complexity. In R. L. Hunter-Anderson (ed.) *Recent Advances in Micronesian Archaeology. Micronesica Supplement* 2: 137–152.

Petersen, G. 1999 Sociopolitical rank and conical clanship in the Caroline Islands. *Journal of the Polynesian Society* 108: 367–410.

Phillips, T. 2003 Seascapes and landscapes in Orkney and northern Scotland. *World Archaeology* 35: 371–384.

Pollard, T. 1999 The drowned and the saved: archaeological perspectives on the sea as grave. In J. Downes and T. Pollard (eds.) *The Loved Body's Corruption: Archaeological contributions to the study of human mortality.* 30–51. Cruithne Press: Glasgow.

Price, T. D. 2000 The introduction of farming in northern Europe. In T. D. Price (ed.) *Europe's First Farmers.* 260–300. Cambridge University Press: Cambridge.

Pryor, F. 2004 Some thoughts on boats as Bronze Age artefacts. In P. Clark (ed.) *The Dover Bronze Age Boat in Context: Society and water transport in prehistoric Europe.* 31–34. Oxbow: Oxford.

Rainbird, P. 1999a Islands out of time: towards a critique of island archaeology. *Journal of Mediterranean Archaeology* 12: 216–234.

Rainbird P. 1999b Entangled biographies: western Pacific ceramics and the tombs of Pohnpei. *World Archaeology* 31: 214–224.

Rainbird, P. 2002a A message for our future? The Rapa Nui (Easter Island) ecodisaster and Pacific island environments. *World Archaeology* 33: 436–451.

Rainbird, P. 2002b Making sense of petroglyphs: the sound of rock-art. In B. David and M. Wilson (eds.) *Inscribed Landscapes: Marking and making place.* 93–103. University of Hawaii Press: Honolulu.

Rainbird, P. 2003 Taking the *tapu*: defining Micronesia by absence. *Journal of Pacific History* 38: 237–250.

Rainbird, P. 2004 *The Archaeology of Micronesia.* Cambridge University Press: Cambridge.

Rainbird, P. 2006 The archaeology of the conical clan in Micronesia. In I. Lilley (ed.) *Archaeology of Oceania: Australia and the Pacific Islands.* 302–317. Blackwell: Oxford.

Rainbird, P. in press The role of fishing lure shanks for the past people of Pohnpei, eastern Caroline Islands, Micronesia. In A. Anderson, K. Green and F. Leach (eds.) *Vastly Ingenious: Essays on oceanic material culture.* University of Otago Press: Dunedin.

Rainbird, P. forthcoming The body and the senses: implications for landscape archaeology. In B. David and J. Thomas (eds.) *The Handbook of Landscape Archaeology.* Left Coast Press: Walnut Creek, Cal.

Rainbird, P. and Wilson, M. 2002 Crossing the line: the enveloped cross in Pohnpei, Federated States of Micronesia. *Antiquity* 76: 635–636.

Ray, H. P. 2003 *The Archaeology of Seafaring in Ancient South Asia.* Cambridge University Press: Cambridge.

Ray, K. 2004 Axes, kula, and things that were 'good to think' in the Neolithic of the Irish Sea regions. In V. Cummings and C. Fowler (eds.) *The Neolithic of the Irish Sea: Materiality and traditions of practice.* 160–173. Oxbow: Oxford.

Renfrew, C. 2004 Islands out of time? Towards an analytical framework. In S. Fitzpatrick (ed.) *Voyages of Discovery: The archaeology of islands.* 275–294. Praeger: Westport, Conn.

Richards, C. 1996 Henges and water: towards an elemental understanding of monumentality and landscape in late Neolithic Britain. *Journal of Material Culture* 1: 313–336.

Robb, J. 2001 Island identities: ritual, travel and the creation of difference in Neolithic Malta. *European Journal of Archaeology* 4: 175–202.

Roberts, O. 2004 Round the headland or over the horizon? An examination of evidence for British prehistoric efforts to construct a seaworthy boat. In P. Clark (ed.) *The Dover Bronze Age Boat in Context: Society and water transport in prehistoric Europe.* 35–50. Oxbow: Oxford.

Rockman, M. 2003 Knowledge and learning in the archaeology of colonization. In M. Rockman and J. Steele (eds.) *Colonization of Unfamiliar Landscapes: The archaeology of adaptation.* 3–24. Routledge: London.

Rolett, B. V. 2002 Voyaging and interaction in Ancient East Polynesia. *Asian Perspectives* 41: 182–194.

Rowley-Conwy, P. and Storå, J. 1997 Pitted Ware seals and pigs from Ajvide, Gotland: methods of study and first results. In G. Burenhult (ed.) *Remote Sensing, Vol. I: Osteo-anthropological, economic, environmental and technical analyses.* 113–125. *Stockholm University Theses and Papers in North-European Archaeology,* 13a.

Said, E. 1978 *Orientalism.* Routledge and Keegan Paul: London.

Sauer, C. O. 1968 *Northern Mists.* Turtle Island Foundation: San Francisco.

Scarre, C. 2002 Coast and cosmos: the Neolithic monuments of northern Brittany. In C. Scarre (ed.) *Monuments and Landscape in Atlantic Europe: Perception and society during the Neolithic and Bronze Age.* 84–102. Routledge: London.

Schulting, R., Tresset, A. and Dupont, C. 2004 From harvesting the sea to stock rearing along the Atlantic façade of north-west Europe. *Environmental Archaeology* 9: 143–154.

Shakespeare, W. 1987 *The Tempest.* Oxford University Press: Oxford.

Sharp, A. 1963 *Ancient Voyagers in Polynesia.* Angus and Robertson: Sydney.

Sharp, N. 1996 *Reimagining Sea Space in History and Contemporary Life: Pulling up some old anchors.* The Australian National University, North Australian Research Unit Discussion Paper 5.

Sharples, N. 2000 Antlers and Orcadian rituals: an ambiguous role for red deer in Neolithic Orkney. In A. Ritchie (ed.) *Neolithic Orkney in its European Context.* 107–116. McDonald Institute Monographs: Cambridge.

Sheridan, A. 2003a French connections I: spreading the *marmites* thinly. In I. Armit, E. Murphy, E. Nelis and D. Simpson (eds.) *Neolithic Settlement in Ireland and Western Britain.* 3–17. Oxbow: Oxford.

Sheridan, A. 2003b Ireland's earliest 'passage' tombs: a French connection? In G. Burenhult (ed.) *Stones and Bones: Formal disposal of the dead in Atlantic Europe during the Mesolithic-Neolithic interface 6000–3000 BC.* 9–15. *British Archaeological Reports, International Series,* 1201.

Skaarup, J. 1995 Stone-Age burials in boats. In O. Crumlin-Pedersen and B. M. Thye (eds.) *The Ship as Symbol in Prehistoric and Medieval Scandinavia.* 51–58. *Publications of the National Museum (Copenhagen), Studies in Archaeology and History,* 1.

Smith, B. 1989 *European Vision and the South Pacific.* 2nd edition. Oxford University Press: Oxford.

Smith, B. 1992 *Imagining the Pacific: In the wake of the Cook voyages.* Melbourne University Press: Melbourne.

Spennemann, D. 2005 Traditional and nineteenth century communication patterns in the Marshall Islands. *Micronesian Journal of the Humanities and Social Sciences* 4: 25–52.

Spriggs, M. 1996 Early agriculture and what went before in Island Melanesia. In D. R. Harris (ed.) *The Origins and Spread of Agriculture and Pastoralism in Eurasia.* 524–537. University College, London Press: London.

Spriggs, M. 1997 *The Island Melanesians.* Blackwell: Oxford.

Stevenson, R. L. 1886 *Kidnapped.* Collins: London.

Stocking, G. W. Jr. 1987 *Victorian Anthropology.* Free Press: New York.

Stoddart, S. 2002 Monuments in the pre-historic landscape of the Maltese islands ritual and domestic transformations. In B. David and M. Wilson (eds.) *Inscribed Landscapes: Marking and making place.* 176–186. University of Hawaii Press: Honolulu.

Stoddart, S., Bonanno, A., Gouder, T., Malone, C. and Trump, D. 1993 Cult in an island society: prehistoric Malta in the Tarxien period. *Cambridge Archaeological Journal* 3: 3–19.

Sutton, D. E. 2001 *Remembrance of Repasts: An anthropology of food and memory.* Berg: Oxford.

Terrell, J. E. 2004 Island models of reticulate evolution: the 'ancient lagoons' hypothesis. In S. Fitzpatrick (ed.) *Voyages of Discovery: The archaeology of islands.* 203–222. Praeger: Westport, Conn.

Thomas, C. 1985 *Exploration of a Drowned Landscape: Archaeology and history of the Isles of Scilly.* Batsford: London.

Thomas, C. 1994 *And Shall These Mute Stones Speak? Post-Roman Inscriptions in Western Britain.* University of Wales Press: Cardiff.

Thomas, N. 1989 The force of ethnology. *Current Anthropology* 30: 27–34.

Thomas, N. 1991 *Entangled Objects: Exchange, material culture, and colonialism in the Pacific.* Harvard University Press: Cambridge, Mass.

Tilley, C. 1994 *A Phenomenology of Landscape: Places, paths and monuments.* Berg: Oxford.

Tilley, C. 1999 *Metaphor and Material Culture.* Blackwell: Oxford.

Tilley, C. 2004 *The Materiality of Stone: Explorations in landscape phenomenology.* Berg: Oxford.

Torrence, R. 1993 Ethnoarchaeology, museum collections and prehistoric exchange: obsidian-tipped artifacts from the Admiralty Islands. *World Archaeology* 24: 467–481.

Tresset, A. 2003 French connections II: of cows and men. In I. Armit, E. Murphy, E. Nelis and D. Simpson (eds.) *Neolithic Settlement in Ireland and Western Britain.* 18–30. Oxbow: Oxford.

Trump, D. 2002 *Malta: Prehistory and temples.* Midsea: Valletta.

van Andel, T. H. and Runnels, C. 1987 *Beyond the Acropolis.* Stanford University Press: Stanford.

Van de Noort, R. 2004 An ancient seascape: the social context of seafaring in the Bronze Age. *World Archaeology* 35: 404–415.

Waldren, J. 2002 Conceptions of the Mediterranean: islands of the mind. In W. Waldren and J. Ensenyat (eds.) *World Islands in Prehistory: International insular investigations.* 1–6. British Archaeological Reports International Series 1095.

Waldren, W. and Ensenyat, J. (eds.) 2002 *World Islands in Prehistory: International insular investigations.* British Archaeological Reports International Series 1095.

Wallin, P. and Martinsson-Wallin, H. 1997 Osteological analysis of skeletal remains from a megalithic grave at Ansarve, Tofta Parish, Gotland. In

G. Burenhult (ed.) *Remote Sensing, Vol. I: Osteo-anthropological, economic, environmental and technical analyses.* 23–28. *Stockholm University Theses and Papers in North-European Archaeology,* 13a.

Weisler, M. 1998 Hard evidence for prehistoric interaction in Polynesia. *Current Anthropology* 39: 521–532.

Westerdahl, C. 1992 The maritime cultural landscape. *The International Journal of Nautical Archaeology* 21: 5–14.

Westerdahl, C. 1994 Maritime cultures and ship types: brief comments on the significance of maritime archaeology. *The International Journal of Nautical Archaeology* 23: 265–270.

Westerdahl, C. 2005 Seal on land, elk at sea: notes on and applications of the ritual landscape of the seaboard. *The International Journal of Nautical Archaeology* 34: 2–23.

White, J. P. 2004 Where the wild things are: prehistoric animal translocation in the circum New Guinea archipelago. In S. Fitzpatrick (ed.) *Voyages of Discovery: The archaeology of islands.* 147–164. Praeger: Westport, Conn.

White, J. P., Clark, G. and Bedford, S. 2000 Distribution, present and past, of *Rattus praetor* in the Pacific and its implications. *Pacific Science* 54: 105–117.

Whittle, A. 1996 *Europe in the Neolithic: The creation of new worlds.* Cambridge University Press: Cambridge.

Woodcock, J. 2004 The early Bronze Age on the Isle of Man: back into the mainstream? In V. Cummings and C. Fowler (eds.) *The Neolithic of the Irish Sea: Materiality and traditions of practice.* 214–223. Oxbow: Oxford.

Wooding, J. 1996 *Communication and Commerce along the Western Sealanes AD 400–800.* British Archaeological Reports International Series 654.

Wooding, J. 2001 St Brendan's boat: dead hides and the living sea in Columban and related hagiography. In J. Carey, M. Herbert and P.Ó Riain (eds.) *Studies in Irish Hagiography. Saints and Scholars.* 77–92. Four Courts Press: Dublin.

Woodman, P. 2000 Getting back to the basics: transitions to farming in Ireland and Britain. In T. D. Price (ed.) *Europe's First Farmers.* 219–259. Cambridge University Press: Cambridge.

Woodman, P. and McCarthy, M. 2003 Contemplating some awful(ly) interesting vistas: importing cattle and red deer into prehistoric Ireland. In I. Armit, E. Murphy, E. Nelis and D. Simpson (eds.) *Neolithic Settlement in Ireland and Western Britain.* 31–39. Oxbow: Oxford.

Woolner, D. 1957 Graffiti of ships at Tarxien, Malta. *Antiquity* 31: 60–67.

Zammit, T. Sir 1930 *Prehistoric Malta: The Tarxien temples.* Oxford University Press: Oxford.

Zvelebil, M. 1986 Mesolithic societies and the transition to farming: problems of time, scale and organisation. In M. Zvelebil (ed.) *Hunters in Transition:*

Mesolithic societies of temperate Eurasia and their transition to farming. 167–188. Cambridge University Press: Cambridge.

Zvelebil, M. 1996 The agricultural frontier and the transition to farming in the circum-Baltic region. In D. Harris (ed.) *The Origins and Spread of Agriculture and Pastoralism in Eurasia.* 323–345. University College, London Press: London.

Zvelebil, M. and Lillie, M. 2000 Transition to agriculture in eastern Europe. In T. D. Price (ed.) *Europe's First Farmers.* 57–92. Cambridge University Press: Cambridge.

Index